CW00493983

World Leader in
Steam & Fluid control

spirax/sarco

Spirax Sarco Korea Ltd.

Jung Woo Bldg. 3F 1552-8, Seocho-Dong
Seocho-Gu, Seoul, 137-873, Korea
Tel. 82-2-3489-9777 / 82-2-525-5755
Fax. 82-2-525-5766 Mobile. 011-780-2167
E-mail. wookchang@kr.spiraxsarco.com

DYNAMIC KOREA

Korea Plus

Seoul, Korea

Gyeongbok Palace is the most representative palace of the Joseon dynasty. Built on a small island in a lotus pond, autumn is the perfect time to enjoy Hyangwonjeong.

Sungnye Gate, nestled low between high-rise buildings, serves as the gateway to the capital city of Seoul. It is a 600-year-old wooden structure that was built in 1398, after King Taejo founded the Joseon dynasty and moved the capital from Gegyung to Hanyang (today's Seoul).

200
B
162
B

Dynamic KOREA

Translated by Lee Don-hee and Yoon Yeon-hae

Published by Korea Plus
521-201 Jugong Apartment,
131 Sangil-dong, Gangdong-gu, Seoul 134-795, Korea
Phone: (82 2) 442-8084 Fax: (82 2) 427-8084
http://www.korea-plus.net e-mail: lilybu@korea.com

First printing, 2005

Printed in Korea by Samsung Moonhwa Printing Co., Ltd.
Phone: (82 2) 468-0361~5 Fax: (82 2) 461-6798

ISBN: 89-956831-0-4

CONTENTS

Preface

The national image of Korea, which has long symbolized the country, has undergone many changes recently. Once called "The Land of the Morning Calm" and "The Courteous Country of the East," the Republic of Korea was known for kimchi and ginseng for quite some time before it became known as a high-tech powerhouse.

These days, countries as well as individuals and companies endeavor to enhance their images. With this in mind, the Korean government has released a new national logo design, "*Dynamic Korea*." The new logo represents a contemporary interpretation of the traditional Korean pattern, taegeuk (yin and yang), which symbolizes change, innovation, self-confidence and a dynamic future.

Now is the time for Koreans to work together to establish a world-class national brand image. As part of such an effort, I put together *Dynamic Korea* because it contains vivid images of all parts of Korea today, from the cities to the countryside to the islands that surround the peninsula. This book also has many photographs of the nation's unpolluted natural landscape and traditional culture.

I am hopeful that *Dynamic Korea* will open up people's minds to the potential that Korea holds, helping everyone who reads it to better understand the country and its people.

Woopo is the largest primal wetland in Korea, and still retains the mysteries of ancient times. Located in Changnyeong County, South Gyeongsang province, it hosts many indigenous species of flora and fauna that have remained undisturbed since people started living here thousands of years ago. Residents make their living by fishing snails from unpolluted swamp areas.

The grand concert of Korean drums, where brilliant dance movements and the magnificence of the scale set off this percussion festival.

Korea, a Long History, a Bright Future

The Republic of Korea, or Korea is it's more commonly known, is a democratic republic located on the Korean peninsula in Northeast Asia. The Korean people are an ethnicity onto their own, and trace their roots back to Mongol tribes. Korea has maintained a homogenous nation since the era of Old Joseon, Korea's first state. The record describing Dangun, the mythical founder of the Korean people, appears in *Samguk Yusa*, a collection of legends and a history of the Three Kingdoms of ancient Korea, written by a Buddhist monk, Ilyeon, during the reign of King Chungryol (1206-1289) in the Goryeo dynasty. The story goes as follows.

Once upon a time, Hwan-ung, the son of the heavenly god, yearned to fulfill the ideal of Hongik Ingan (providing humans with great happiness). As such, he descended to the top of Mt. Taebaek, to a divine-alter tree called Sindansu, along with his ministers of clouds, rain and wind, and carrying three cheonbuin, or God-given seals of king. He named the place Sinsi, City of God, and ruled over 360 human affairs, such as farming, death, disease, punishment, good and evil. Sometime after arriving, a bear and a tiger who were living in a cave together came to Hwan-ung and asked to be turned into humans. Upon hearing their wishes, Hwan-ung gave them a bundle of mugwort and cloves of garlic. He then told them to return to their cave, to eat only the food he had given them and to stay out of the sunlight for 100 days. The tiger, unable to endure such conditions, gave up and left the cave, but the bear remained true and in the end became a woman. The bear-woman married Hwan-ung and gave birth to a handsome son, Dangun. Then, in 2,333 B.C., Dangun founded the Ko Joseon kingdom (Old Joseon kingdom), setting up its capital in Asadal (today's Pyeongyang).

There are several diverse interpretations coming out of this founding mythology by Dangun thanks to studies by many scholars over the years. As the myth contains elements of the nation's independent and everlasting spirit, the Dangun mythology has served as a driving force that unites Korean people from all faiths and walks of life, helping them overcome any and all hardships and trials. Furthermore, throughout the modern age, the Dangun mythology has constantly functioned as the traditional and cultural basis of the Korean people.

Korea's first Three Tribal Kingdoms, Goguryeo, Baekje and Silla, were founded as early as the 1st century A.D. By 700 A.D, Silla took over the other two kingdoms and unified Korea as a single nation. The Unified Silla kingdom ruled and prospered for some 250 years. In the 9th century, it was divided into Silla, Hubaekje (later Baekje) and Hugoguryeo (later Goguryeo), ushering in a period known as the Later Three Kingdoms of Korea. It was in the early 10th century that the Goryeo dynasty unified Korea again. Later, the Mongol Empire, founded by Genghis Khan, invaded Goryeo. After Goryeo's collapse, the Joseon dynasty was founded in the late 14th century. There were also foreign invasions during the 500-odd-year-long rule of the Joseon dynasty, including the Hideyoshi invasions of 1592-98, and Byongja Horan, the Manchu invasion of 1636. With Japan's annexaiton of the country in 1910, Korea was put under colonial rule for 36 years. Korea was persistent in its independence movements at home and abroad, though, especially those coordinated by the Korean Provisional Government in Shanghai. On August 15, 1945, following Japan's surrender at the end of World War II, Korea was finally liberated and gained independence.

However, Korea's independence brought about as much joy and happiness as it did political, economic and social upheaval. In the wake of the Second World War, the U.S. and the Soviet Union occupied the south and the north, respectively, of the Korean peninsula. The 38th parallel was designated as the demarcation line between the two countries' spheres of influence, with the U.S. and the Soviet Union each establishing military administrations on the Korean peninsula. As a result, the Koreans, far from achieving their actual independence, came to face national division. The aspirations of the Korean people for independence eventually reached the United Nations (UN), and in 1947, the second UN General Assembly proposed holding simultaneous general elections in North and South Korea under the supervision of UN monitoring delegations. But with the opposition of North Korea, South Korea alone had to hold general elections in 1948, establishing the country's National Assembly. The first Korean parliament was then set up and promulgated the Constitution of the Republic of Korea, inheriting the tradition of the Korean Provisional Government, and declared its establishment at home and abroad, taking a first step as a free democratic nation. The UN recognized Korea as the sole legitimate government on the Korean Peninsula. Two years later, in 1950, North Korea invaded South Korea, and the war ended with an armistice agreement signed by the U.S.-led and ROK-supported UN Command and the North Korean Army and Chinese People's Volunteers on July 27, 1953. The Korean War, which lasted three years and one month, left the Korean peninsula in ruins.

In April 1954, a political conference was held in Geneva to resolve the Korean problem in accordance with the Articles of the armistice agreement, but it broke down just two months later, resulting in the continued division of the Korean Peninsula with the armistice line, not the 38th parallel, as the official demarcation line. Until now, more than 50 years after the armistice, the Korean peninsula has remained divided, with a democratic government in the South and a communist regime in the North.

With the start of the new millennium, an atmosphere of reconciliation was created between the two Koreas, raising hopes for reunification among the Korean people. In particular, there has been increasing inter-Korean exchanges, including the reunions of families separated by the Korean War, the opening of Mt. Geumgang in North Korea to tourism, and the construction of an industrial complex in Gaeseong, North Korea, in which South Korean companies are producing goods.

Until the second half of the 1940s, Korea exported mostly marine products, such as agar-agar, fresh fish and dried fish because of a lack of industrial infrastructure. Beginning in the 1950s, however, mineral products, including tungsten, graphite, and iron ore, emerged as Korea's major exports. After 1961, when exports started to pick up steam, the volume of primary light industry goods, such as plywood, garments, wigs and shoes manufactured by small and mid-size companies, increased greatly.

In 1964, Korean exports surpassed $100 million and in 1969, riding on the wave of the world's economic boom, Korea, no longer an underdeveloped country, achieved an astonishing annual export growth rate of 41% and became a developing country. At the start of the 1970s, Korea started to promote policies aimed at developing heavy chemical industries, including the manufacture of electronics, steel, petrochemicals, and ships, in a large-scale manner. As a result, Korea was able to attain $10 billion in exports by 1977, mainly due to a construction boom in the Middle East. In the 1990s, semiconductors, automobiles, ships, chemical products, electric and electronic goods, and machinery emerged as Korea's main export goods. In 1997, though, Korea faced a national crisis touched off by an unprecedented financial crisis in Asia that placed the country under the supervision of the International Monetary Fund (IMF). In the wake of this, Koreans tightened their purse strings and launched a series of nationwide frugality campaigns, uniting the whole nation more than ever before. Koreans actively joined campaigns to collect U.S. dollars and gold in order to help the government repay its foreign debts, displaying the people's great perseverance in overcoming a national hardship and their potential to strengthen national competitiveness. In late 2004, Korea saw its exports soar to $250 billion, a fact that is nothing short of miraculous given that it was accomplished amid stagnant domestic demand and fierce international competition.

Korea is no longer the poor and powerless country that it used to be. The Seoul Asian Games in 1986, the Seoul Olympic Games in 1988, and the Busan Asian Games in 2002, all of which were dedicated to the harmony and advancement of humanity, allowed Korea to take big strides on the world stage. In fact, the opening ceremony of the Seoul Olympics, as evidenced by an Associated Press (AP) article that praised it as a "harmony of Korean mysticism and ultramodern splendor," left a stunning impression on the whole world by unifying the colors, spirit and thoughts of the country and its people. Korea ended up finishing fourth in the medal standings at the Seoul Olympics, with 12 gold, 10 silver and 11 bronze medals.

Korea wished to open the new millennium by co-hosting the football World Cup with Japan in 2002. This was an ambitious challenge. Raising the flag of a new Asia high into the blue sky, Korea and Japan put aside their historical differences and joined hands to emerge as the new leaders of the future.

In December 1997, the 21st session of UNESCO's World Heritage Committee was held at Piazza Del Plebiscito, in Naples, Italy. The annual meeting, attended by some 100 representatives from member countries, was deliberating on 46 cultural properties from 25 countries to see if they deserved to be placed on the UNESCO's World Heritage list. One by one representatives from each country explained the value of their own cultural properties in an eloquent manner by presenting relevant documents and slides. In the end that year, Korea had two places voted onto the World Heritage list unanimously, Changdeok Palace and Hwaseong Fortress in Suwon.

The World Heritage Committee recognized the greatness of Changdeok Palace's architecture, acknowledging the fact that it closely conforms to the uneven topography of the land while its harmonious integration with the surrounding natural landscape is an exceptional example of Far Eastern palace architecture and design. On the other hand, Hwaseong Fortress in Suwon was praised as an outstanding example of early modern military architecture, incorporating the most highly developed features of that period's science from both the East and the West, as illustrated by its strong defensive structure, which was constructed in a scientific, logical and practical fashion.

It was not the first time that Korean cultural properties had been recognized by the world. Seokguram Buddhist Grotto, the *Tripitaka Koreana* at Haein Temple and Jongmyo Shrine were inscribed on the World Heritage list in 1995. In addition, the historic areas around Gyeongju, plus the Gochang, Hwasun and Gangwha Dolmen sites were also added in December 2000, making Korea one of the leading countries on UNESCO's World Heritage list.

Traditional Korean dancing and folk games combined with song and dance are another integral part of the culture. Koreans have long carried on their traditions and unique spirit in tune with the distinct rhythms of their traditional songs and dances. Cultural heritages are a mirror of time. Korean cultural heritages, like the country's gently rolling hills and streams, have gently withstood the abrasion of time and have functioned as a mirror of Korea's past, present and future. Korea has four seasons which show distinct differences: the spring with its bright sunshine and fresh greenery, the summer a with boiling hot sun and lush greenery, the fall with cool breezes and blue skies, and the winter with white snow. It is not easy to find a country with more distinct and beautiful seasonal distinctions than Korea.

A member of the Organization for Economic Cooperation and Development (OECD), Korea has been showing the best performance in exports even while amidst a prolonged economic slump. Samsung Electronics and LG Electronics, two world-class high-tech companies, have been significantly strengthening their brand values by showing off a series of state-of-the-art products, allowing IT powerhouse Korea to continue to bask in an export boom. Lately, Samsung Electronics has developed and marketed a 5-million pixel camera phone and a portable wide-screen TV that can receive Digital Multimedia Broadcasting (DMB), the first of its kind in the world, while LG Electronics has mass produced a 71-inch PDP TV for the first time, following its development of the world's first 50-inch LCD TV.

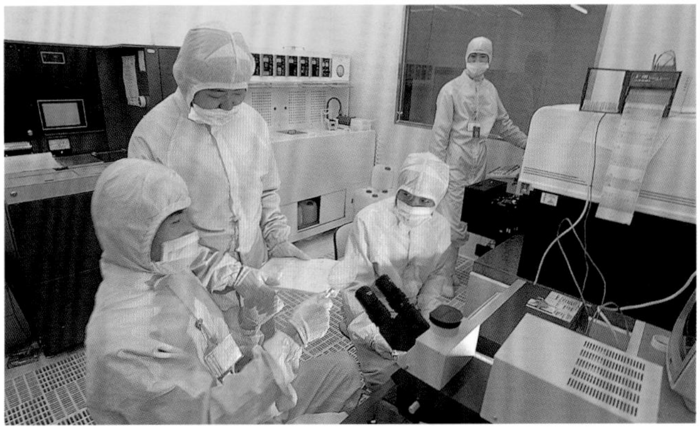

According to a survey released in December 2004 by the OECD of 280,000 15-year-old students in 41 principal industrialized countries, Korea ranked first in terms of how well students tackle problems encountered in everyday life that are not obviously linked to knowledge gained at school. Furthermore, Korea ranked second in reading, third in math, and fourth in science. This outcome was released when the OECD issued its Program for International Student Assessment (PISA) for 2003, a survey carried out once every three years that assesses how far students near the end of compulsory education have acquired certain knowledge and skills.

You will notice the "Made In Korea" labels wherever you go around the world. And Korean youngsters, ranked top in the world in terms of problem solving, will emerge prominently as global leaders of the 21st century.

Seoul has a population of over 10 million people. A walk around Sungnye Gate, originally a grand entrance to Hanyang, the capital of the Joseon dynasty, and the royal palaces of the kingdom, now surrounded by high-rise buildings, allows you to appreciate the harmonized beauty of tradition and modernity. A complete view of Changgyeong Palace

Seoul, Truly A World-Class City

Seoul is a beautiful city where tradition and modernity coexist in a very special way. It is a pleasant, convenient and people-oriented city with brisk economic activity, and is now being reborn as the hub of Northeast Asia. The capital city of the Republic of Korea, Seoul has grown into a teeming metropolis with a population of over 10 million people. Having had to overcome many difficulties over the ages, from foreign invasions to the Japanese occupation to the Korean War and national division, Seoul is now functioning as and playing the role of an international city on a par with other prominent global cities. This has been done primarily on the strength of its rapid economic growth, referred to by many as "The miracle on the Han River." Situated in the middle of the Korean peninsula, Seoul is 605.4 km^2, with the distance between its eastern and western boundaries spanning 36.78 km^2 and the distance between the northern and southern ones spanning 30.3 km^2.

Seoul's population stood at just over 10 million as of the end of 2004. This means that 25% of Korea's population lives in Seoul, even though it represents only 6% of Korea's total land area. Seoul, which means "capital" in Korean, was officially given its name in 1946, after liberation from Japanese colonial rule in 1945. One other interesting fact about Seoul is that it is the only city in the world whose meaning is "capital" and is actually the capital of a country.

Seoul is surrounded by 17 mountains, the highest of which is Mt. Bukhan (836 m). The Han River, a major symbol of Seoul, flows through the middle of the city, supplying drinking water and water for other household and industrial uses to the city's residents. It was during the Neolithic period, some 6,000 years ago, that people started to live around the Han River, which is why many relics of this age have been found around the area. Amsa-dong Prehistoric Settlement Site at Gangdong-gu is the largest group-housing site of the Neolithic period in Korea. During this prehistoric age, people mostly dug deep pits in the ground and built mud huts around them. Amsa-dong mud huts are located in a broad plane along the Han River. This displays how the people at that time depended heavily on fishing. This hypothesis is supported by fishing nets, spears

and other such items that have been excavated in the area.

Upon the founding of the Joseon dynasty in 1392, the founding king, Taejo, or Yi Seonggye as he was known before his ascension to the throne, wanted to move the capital to Hanyang (today's Seoul). After carefully examining the topography of Hanyang, Chong To-jon and other officials produced complete plans and blueprints on how to build Jongmyo (royal ancestral shrines), Sajik-tan (national altar to worship the gods of land and grain), palace buildings, market places and road networks, all in harmony with the surrounding environment.

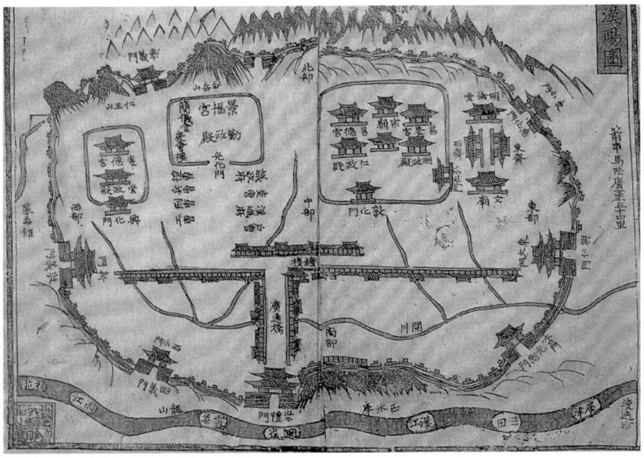

Following the annexation of Korea by Japan in 1910, Seoul was renamed Kyongsong, but it regained its name with liberation in 1945. In 1948, when the government of the Republic of Korea was established, Seoul was designated as its capital. The following year, Seoul was elevated to the status of a Special City and placed directly under the control of the central government. North Korea, on the other hand, designated Seoul as its constitutional capital and Pyeongyang as a temporary capital. For this reason, when the Korean War broke out in 1950, North and South Korea scrambled hard to have Seoul in their possession, reducing it to piles of debris as a result. At the end of the war, many who were part of the UN's forces thought that Seoul was nothing but a "poor and hopeless city."

However, as social and economic conditions improved, Seoul was able to transform itself from a "horizontal city" into a "vertical city," with large numbers of tall buildings and skyscrapers. In addition, with an increasing number of factories and businesses springing up, Seoul came to function as the backbone of the country's economic growth.

Gyeongbok Palace, the primary residence for the royal family of the Joseon dynasty, was picked as people's favorite tourist spot in a recent survey with foreign visitors by the Seoul Metropolitan government. Gyeongbok Palace is very special because it allows visitors to experience 500 years of Joseon dynasty history in one place.

Seoul Tower is located on top of Mt. Nam, or Namsan as Koreans say, and is a major landmark in this capital city. It was ranked as the second most popular tourist destination in Seoul. Visiting Namsan's observation tower allows people to see all of Seoul and the surrounding areas in one panoramic view. There are many other must-see attractions in Seoul, including Dongdaemoon and Namdaemoon shopping districts; plenty of must-eat food, such as bulgogi, kimchi and bibimbop; and a great many must-see performances, including the traditional Royal Guard Changing Ceremony, a reenactment of the changing of the royal guards of the Joseon dynasty. There is also Nanta, a non-verbal performance of amazing rhythms that dramatizes customary Korean percussion in a strikingly comedic stage show, and the Insa-dong Festival, which features Korean musical instruments and regional dishes.

Seoul's air transportation volume, a barometer of a city's openness and globalization, has surpassed 10 million people. The city's hosting of the Olympics in 1988 had a hugely positive impact on the way the rest of the world viewed Seoul and its people. In addition, by successfully hosting the Europe-Asia Meeting (ASEM), which brought together leaders from 26 European and Asian countries, Seoul secured an opportunity to grow into an international convention city. In particular, Seoul has become more internationally known after it successfully co-hosted the 2002 World Cup of football with Japan, when fans and members of the "Red Devils," the official fan club of the Korean national soccer team, flooded Seoul's City Hall plaza, the streets of Seoul, and other major cities in red clothing whenever Korea played, proudly waving the national flag, Taegeukki.

The capital city of Korea, Seoul has transformed itself from a "horizontal city" into a "vertical city," with large numbers of high-rise buildings and skyscrapers. Seoul has served as the backbone of the nation's economic growth as many domestic and foreign companies do brisk business in the region.

Seoul's City Hall plaza has turned into a favorite place for both young and old residents of the city. It is now a common sight to see people relaxing on the grass of the oblong-shaped area just in front of City Hall. In the summer, kids can have fun trying to dodge the jets of water from the plaza's fountain, and in winter skating on the ice rink that is built there.

Myeong-dong, located in the heart of Seoul, is the city's hippest fashion district, offering all the latest fashion trends. From every alley and side street you'll hear the latest pop music, adding to the allure of the area that teems with liveliness and youth, making it the "fashion heaven" of Korea.

Insa-dong is a lovely street tucked away from the hustle and bustle of central Seoul. Often called "the face of Seoul," it is frequently visited by foreign tourists. This small street in downtown Seoul is replete with stores selling traditional Korean items, such as ceramics, old paintings, brassware, and many other relics of the past. Visitors can get a glimpse of Korea's cultural heritage through its assortment of priceless antiques.

Yeouido is really a city within the city. It is the center of politics and finance, and home to the National Assembly, the financial district, the major television networks and the nation's largest banks. On weekends, people can ride their bikes or go rollerblading through the vast recreational plaza in the middle of the small island.

한화증권
한화증권
Prudential Financial

The Convention and Exhibition (COEX) center in Samsung-dong, southern Seoul, served as a stepping-stone for Seoul to grow into an international convention city. The first ASEM summit of the new millennium, which brought together 26 heads of states and leaders from Asia and Europe, was held at the COEX center, becoming the biggest international conference ever held in Korea.

Many people take advantage of the Han River by using it for water sports or simply to relax. Han River ferry cruises are an especially memorable event at night, when the river area is at its most beautiful and the pleasant breeze coming off the water makes it thoroughly enjoyable.

Bridges over the Han River have long been playing a pivotal role in the lives of Seoul's citizens. Since the Han Iron Bridge was built in 1900, the first bridge to span the mighty Han River, as many as 29 bridges, ranging from Paldang Bridge at the upper reaches of the Han River to Gimpo Bridge at its lower reaches, have been built on the strength of Korea's rapid economic development. In order to boost the nation's tourism revenue and vitalize the economy by highlighting the beauty of Seoul, the Seoul City government has lights illuminate the bridges at night, breathing vitality into the city.

A major symbol of Seoul, the Han River is called the "lifeline" for Korea because it has made the central region of the Korean peninsula fertile and rich for so long. It has also contributed greatly to the nation's cultural development over the years, enabling Seoul to emerge prominently as the center of politics, economy and culture in Korea. The Han River is approximately 514 km long, with its basin measuring 26,219 km^2. The total length of the Han River's tributaries is 7,430 km.

A host of valuable ceremonies, which used to be performed at royal palaces during the Joseon dynasty, are being revived magnificently in order for the public to enjoy.

The Royal Guards Changing Ceremony is presented at the entrance to Deoksu Palace, Gyeongbok Palace, and Changdeok Palace. The guards wear traditional military uniforms and swords, and perform to the beat of drums.

Deep in the heart of downtown Seoul, crowded by a jungle of concrete, there are places that feel like an oasis:royal palaces. These relics from a bygone era are greatly loved for retaining the tranquility and stillness of earlier times amongst the hustle and bustle of modern city life. Everything at Changdeok Palace's Nakseonjae (**left**), from beautiful flower-patterned walls to small footstones below the floors of Korean verandas, was built and decorated meticulously and with great care.
An aerial view of Deoksu Palace (**top above**) .
Geunjeongjeon at Gyeongbok Palace (**above**).

Changdeok Palace epitomizes the essence of traditional Korean architecture, as it shows a complete harmony between nature and people. It was built in 1405 as a detached extension to Gyeongbok Palace by King Taejong (1400-1418), the third monarch of the Joseon dynasty. After the palace's destruction as a result of a fire at Gyeongbok Palace, it was used as the main imperial residence for about 300 years. There are many important old palace buildings remaining in Changdeok Palace, including Nakseonjae and the only royal garden of its kind in Korea, Biwon ("Secret Garden"). Changdeok Palace is inscribed on UNESCO's World Heritage list.

Gyeongbok Palace is the most representative royal palace from the Joseon dynasty, and is replete with a history that is over 500 years old. Amisan Garden (**above**) in the back of Gangnyeongjeon, once the bedchamber of the king and queen, has tiers on which flowers and plants have been placed with decorative rocks, and a chimney with designs inlaid with brick and granite sculptural objects, creating a relaxed and peaceful atmosphere throughout the year.

Today, thick old trees hang down over the pond that King Kojong had built in 1867 along with Hyangwonjeong, the pavilion whose shadows over the water creates truly picturesque scenes, with pretty water lilies adorning the pond. Hyangwonjeong was originally connected to the north shore of the pond by a bridge. Hyangwonjeong means "fresh fragrances of lotus blossoms spread through the air," while the bridge connecting it to the other side, Chwihyang, means "being intoxicated with the fragrance of lotus blossoms," leading to the conclusion that it must have been full of elegant lotus blossoms in earlier times.

Historical cultural monuments are lit up at night to show off their profound gracefulness, a beauty that is quite distinct from that offered by the myriad dazzling neon signs around them. This illumination breathes new life into old monuments that are trapped in darkness, making the nighttime view of the city stunning.

With the historic opening of the Korean Train Express (KTX), Korea has joined France, Germany, Japan, and Spain as countries that operate super high-speed trains. The opening of the KTX, which is dubbed "a transportation revolution in Korea's 105-year railroad history," will not only bring about enormous changes to the lives of Koreans by enabling them to get anywhere in the country within three hours, but will also play a pivotal role in turning Korea into an economic and logistics hub in Northeast Asia.

A night view of Busan, a port city that aims to become a logistics hub for Northeast Asia.

Korea's Gateway to the Pacific, Busan Is a City of Passion and Romance

Busan has been serving as the gateway to Korea since it was forced to open its port in 1876 by the Japanese. During the three years of the Korean War (1950-53), Busan accommodated the government of the Republic of Korea, serving as the provisional capital city. Today, Busan is the second largest city in Korea, with a population of 4 million people, and connects the Pacific Ocean and the continent of Asia.

It was some 40 years ago that Busan's Haeundae Beach was developed into a sun tanning resort. These days, it's impossible to talk about Korea's great beaches without mentioning Haeundae. When the summer vacation season rolls around, Haeundae is flooded with vacationers flocking from all over the nation, especially in August when the average temperature soars above 30°C and about 300,000 vacationers a day flock to the beach, turning the area into an enormous sea of human beings. So what makes Haeundae Beach so popular? First of all, Haeundae is located in a big city, and so is well equipped with all the amenities that go along with that, including convenient transportation, a wide range of accommodations and leisure and recreational facilities. Furthermore, it is endowed with exceptionally beautiful natural surroundings, white sandy beaches, and clean, shallow seawater. At almost a mile long (1.5 km), and between 30-50 meters in width, Haeundae Beach has a total area of 58,400 m^2. Two of Haeundae's secret gems are Damaji ("moon-viewing") Hill, which offers a spectacular view of the sun rising in the morning and the moon rising over the East Sea in the evening, and Dongbaek Island. Located at the southern tip of Haeundae Beach, Dongbaek Island is a picturesque place, and yet another reason for tourists to come to Haeundae Beach every year.

Gwanganri Beach is especially popular with younger people. Plenty of raw fish restaurants, enchanting cafes, and restaurant-bars all line the seaside road. At night, when parking lots are full of expensive cars, the area turns into a brilliantly illuminated place where scores of people looking their best crowd shops as well as the beach. Yet when dawn breaks, these same people give way to those living in the neighborhood, who come out on the beach to exercise and enjoy the fresh morning sea wind.

Busan also boasts a beautiful coastline. Taejongdae, located on the southern tip of Yeong Island, presents a magnificent view, with 250-meterhigh peculiarly-shaped rugged cliffs dropping straight down to the sea and a decades-old pine tree forest, reminding many who visit of the east end of Mt. Geumgang, North Korea. Ships passing by often blow their horns as if to utter cries of joy and admiration at the fabulous sight. In addition, on Dongbaek and Oryuk Islands, people can enjoy the calm and tranquil atmosphere offered there. Furthermore, Haedong Yonggung ("the palace of the East Sea dragon king") Temple can be seen some 4 km north of Songjeong Beach. Standing on a rocky cliff beside the beach near Daebyon Port, this temple looks like it was taken from a magnificent Oriental painting.

Busan also has many traditional folk games and plays that have been passed down over time, including Dongnae Juldarigi ("tug-of war from Dongnae"), Dongnae Yaryu ("masque drama from Dongnae"), Suyeong Yaryu ("masque drama from Suyeong"), Jwasuyeong Eobangnori ("folk custom for fishing from the west of Suyeong"), the last

three being national Important Intangible Cultural Assets. There is also Suyeong Nongcheong Nori ("farmers' song and dance"), Dongnae Hakchum ("crane dance from Dongnae"), Dongnae Jisin Balgi ("house-to-house visits by a traditional farm music band from Dongnae") and Busan Aminongak ("traditional farm music from Busan"), the last four being local Intangible Cultural Assets. Dongnae Juldarigi, in particular, has been a source of pride among residents of the area because it has one of the longest histories of its kind.

The UN Cemetery was founded to commemorate UN soldiers who lost their lives during the Korean War. About 2,000 soldiers from 21 allied nations are buried in a 13,500 m^2 cemetery. The Korean government granted the land to the UN, in perpetuity, as a tribute to all those who gave their lives in the war, to uphold the cause of peace and freedom. Valuable trees sent from various countries around the world, as well as well-trimmed grass and beautiful flowers, decorate the cemetery.

Beomeo Temple, located on the eastern slope of Mt. Geumjeong in Busan, is one of the three largest temples in the southeastern part of the country. Beomeo Temple's name means "temple of the fish from Nirvana." In order to enter Beomeo Temple, visitors need to pass through Iljumun ("One Pillar Gate," the first gate), the "Gate of the Guardians of the Four Directions" and the "Gate of Non-duality." It is said that as soon as you step through the gates, all of your troubles disappear. After passing these first three gates, you reach the top level, where Daeungjeon "(Main Buddha Hall") and the rest of the compound stand comfortably in the protective arms of the forest, where gingko trees and pine trees that are hundreds of years old stand with branches together, as if to greet visitors, and wind chimes ring softly in the breeze. More than 400 years after it was first built, Daeungjeon still remains graceful and elegant.

Yongdusan Park, standing high on Mt. Yongdu and overlooking the center of Busan, serves as a great place for people to rest and relax. Mt. Yongdu was formerly called Mt. Songhyeon due to its abundant pine trees. Busan Tower, sitting atop Mt. Yongdu, rises 118 meters into the air to form a major landmark of Busan, as it can be seen from any point in the city. The observation deck at the top commands a spectacular view of the metropolitan area and surrounding harbor, which is lined with deep-sea fishing vessels. On a clear day, you can see as far as the Oryuk Islands, Taejongdae, and even Japan's Tsushima Island. The night view is also truly amazing. Finally, Gwangan Bridge, yet another famous tourist attraction, is now acclaimed as a masterpiece of artistic structural work. The bridge, which is equipped with a state-of-the-art illumination system that lights it up with more than 100,000 lightbulbs, makes the night scenery even more beautiful.

Located at the southeastern end of the Korean peninsula, Busan Port is the country's number one port. With its deepwater harbor, the depth changes little with the rise and fall of the tide, an ideal condition for any large port. Through continuous efforts, Busan Port has turned into the modernized harbor of today, the world's fifth largest container port, handling 12 million TEUs per year. As the nation's major port, Busan processes more than 90 percent of all export cargo in Korea. Currently, New Busan Port is being built to enable the simultaneous berth of 30 vessels, and is slated for completion by 2011. By then, Busan Port will stand high as a competitive international harbor. On top of that, Busan is set to host the Asia-Pacific Economic Cooperation (APEC) summit and ministerial meetings in November 2005, and is also is pushing a City Renovation Project under the theme of "Change Busan," all in an effort to transform itself into a competitive global city.

Busan Tower (**above**), a symbol of Busan, is located in Mt. Yongdu ("Dragon Head Hill") Park. Busan Tower has an observatory at its top that commands a spectacular view of the entire city of Busan and the surrounding sea. Having emerged as a popular tourist attraction along with Mt. Yongdu Park, Gwangan Bridge is now acclaimed as a masterpiece of engineering and is equipped with a state-of-the-art illumination system.

As the summer vacation season rolls around, an average of 300,000 vacationers a day flock to Haeundae Beach, turning it into a human sea.

Busan, Korea's second largest city, is Korea's, and the continent of Asia's, first gateway to the Pacific Ocean. In order to prepare itself for the era of the Pacific Rim, and in the face of increasing population growth, Busan is in the midst of building a maritime city that can deal with these challenges properly. Though it has been expanding at a stunning pace for quite sometime, Busan must still transform itself into a city of greater vitality and energy. Behind the shipbuilding yard (**above**) unfolds the city of Busan as a maritime city. A night view of Busan as seen from Busan Tower (**left**).

Jagalchi Fish Market (**top**), known as the "opener of the day" in Busan. From 10 p.m, when inshore and deep-sea fishing boats return to port, to the dawn of the following day, the market thrives with vendors and workers going about their business (**above**). Jagalchi Market's fishery auction opens around 6 a.m., when the market is overflowing with fresh seafood and crowds of merchants flocking from across the nation. Busan Container Port handles 95 percent of Korea's total container traffic (**left**).

The wide open deep blue sea, craggy cliffs and peculiarly-shaped stones that look as if they were carved by a divine hand provide the highlight of most visitors'trip here aboard one of many sightseeing cruises. (**left**) Haedong Yonggung Temple (**top and center**), which stands on a rocky cliff beside the sea, should really be called "The Temple on the Sea." The Oryuk Islands, pride of Busan (**above**).

Clear and resonant sounds echo, as if to drown out the sounds from the rest of the world, when the wind rustles leaves and wild birds flap their wings. Walking through a forest path lined with thick trees on either side, it looks like they are spreading their branches in prayer. The entrance to Tongdo Temple (**left**). Buddhist monks are walking around Geumgan's stairs where jinsinsari ("Buddha's bones") are enshrined (**top**). Beomeo Temple was founded by the great monk Uisang (**above and left**). Student monks take a break from it all (**above and right**).

Anapji was the garden of the Crown Prince's palace. A beautiful artificial pond, Anapji is an excellent example of a garden and lake construction during the Silla period.

Gyeongju, a Millennium of Silla Kingdom History Still Alive and Well

Each and every one of the numerous round tombs that rise up in the city is so huge that they look like small hills from afar. These are the tombs of Silla kings and nobles who, after more than 1,000 years as a kingdom, vanished into the pages of history. Silla was the first kingdom in Korea to unite the various nation states into one country, and its capital, Seorabeol, today's Gyeongju, is a place where the scent of the Silla kingdom's rich and splendid history remains strong.

According to *Samguk Yusa* ("*Memorabilia of the Three Kingdoms*"), the six tribal clans who settled in the Gyeongju plains raised a boy by the name of Pak Hyokkose, who is said to have been born to kingship from an egg so that he could rule the world magnanimously. The Silla kingdom, which began with the birth of Pak Hyokkose near a well named Najeong, at the slope of Mt. Nam, spanned 992 years, or 56 generations, until its demise at Poseokjeong, at the foot of Mt. Nam in today's Gyeongju. More than 1,000 years have passed since the demise of the Silla kingdom, but its history still feels intimately a part of Gyeongju, due in no small measure to the fact that so many relics and artifacts have survived up to two millennia of history.

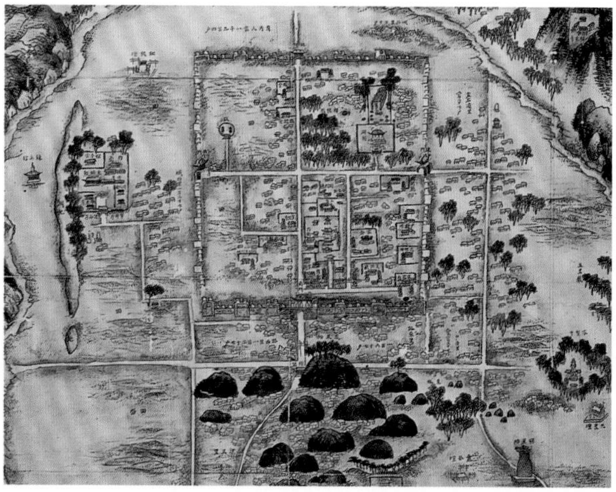

Anapji is an artificial pond that King Munmu, who unified the three Kingdoms into Silla, built in 674 in order to strengthen the dignity of the royal family. As the *Samguk Sagi* ("*History of the Three Kingdoms*") records, Anapji was "a pond...dug within the palace grounds, where artificial mountains were constructed, and flowers, rare birds, and deer raised." Near Anapji are several other important monuments, including Cheomseongdae, Daeneungwon and Gyerim. In fact, Cheomseongdae has been acknowledged as the oldest astronomical observatory and the only stone structure of its kind in Asia. It served as the center of the four main compass directions and the acknowledged meridian during the Silla period. Designated as National Treasure No. 31, Cheomseongdae is divided into three parts: a square stone foundation, a cylinder-shaped tower and the Chinese character 井 (jeong)-shaped top. Its architectural design of harmonizing square- and cylinder-shaped objects represents the traditional Oriental astronomical belief that "sky is round and land square," and that the Chinese character 井 (jeong)-shaped top points exactly in the directions of north, south, east and west.

Daeneungwon is the largest tomb park where ancient tombs from the Silla kingdom are buried. Designated as Historic Site No. 175, Daeneungwon has plenty of diverse-sized tombs of Silla kings and nobles, which range from less than 10 meters long to 120 meters long, and from less than one meter high to 23 meters high. Among other things, Cheonmachong, which to date has yielded upwards of 15,000 relics, including Cheonmado ("mural painting of a flying horse"), is presumed to be the tomb of King Jijeung, the 22nd monarch of Silla.

When combined with Buddhism, Silla art grew to become more exquisite and decorative. In the wake of this, masterpieces such as Bulguksa and Seokguram were created. According to *Samguk Yusa*, the construction of Bulguksa began in 751 and was completed in 774 as a grand Buddhist temple. Bulguksa is clearly the most prominent of any of the ancient structures in terms of architectural value.

Furthermore, along with its architectural splendor, Bulguksa contains the deep and profound truth of Buddhism, inspiring wonder and amazement while symbolizing the "pure Buddha land standing high in the world of suffering, or Sabha." In this sense, Bulguksa can be divided as follows: "this world," which consists of Baegungyo ("Bridge of White Clouds"), Cheongungyo ("Bridge of Blue Clouds"), Jahamun ("Mauve Mist Gate"), Daeungjeon ("Main Sanctuary"), and Museoljeon ("Hall of No Expounding"); "the world to come," which consists of Chilbogyo ("Bridge of Seven Treasures"), Yeonhwagyo ("Lotus Flower Bridge"), and Anyangmun ("Peace Enhancing Gate") Pavilion; and "the past world," which consists of Gwaneumjeon ("Hall of Avalokitesvara") and Birojeon ("Hall of Vairocana").

Overlooking the East Sea, far beyond the ridges of Mt. Toham, is Seokguram, Korea's most famous Buddhist grotto. Designated as National Treasure No. 24, this grotto temple enshrines a 3.48-meter tall statue of a seated Buddha in its center, surrounded by tens of guardian deities, including Palbusinjang ("Eight Congregated Devas"), Inwang ("Benevolent Kings") and Four Heavenly Kings, that are elaborately carved on the stone walls of either side of the entrance and a rectangular antechamber. In addition, the standing image of an 11-headed Gwanseum Bosal, the Goddess of Mercy, is carved on the wall of the rotunda directly behind the central Buddha statue. Inside the rotunda, above the granite panels, are 10 hut-shaped niches, where 10 small statues of bodhisattvas reside, all paying tribute to the Buddha. Seokguram is one of the finest masterpieces of the Unified Silla period, one that is in complete harmony between Buddhist faith and modern architectural skills, and representative of Korea's Buddhist art. Located 30 degrees east-southeast from Seokguram is the underwater tomb of King Munmu, the 30th monarch of the Silla kingdom. It is said that King Munmu ordered that he be cremated and buried in the East Sea after his death so that he could become a dragon to protect Silla. The only submerged burial grounds in the world, the tomb is called Daewangam, or the Great King's Rock, and even today large numbers of people come here to make wishes.

Overlooking Gyeongju, Mt. Nam, or Namsan as it's called in Korean, stands as a proud testimony to one thousand years of the Silla kingdom's brilliant history. Namsan (494 m) was a spiritual refuge for the Silla people, which is why there is a remarkable concentration of outstanding examples of Silla's religious faith and culture there. This area is really an outdoor museum that is comprised of more than 40 valleys, some 100 temples or temple ruins, 80-odd Buddhist statues or carvings and some 60 pagodas, all of which are scattered over the mountainous landscape. These relics remain so intact that Mt. Nam alone is sufficient to discuss Silla's culture.

Namsan was Silla's sacred mountain. The mountain's intrinsic beauty exudes the wonder of nature and the brilliant achievements of the Silla kingdom. Anyone who sets foot here finds it hard to leave. Furthermore, as other precious cultural assets are still thought to be hidden in Namsan, the mountain is acclaimed as a mysterious place whose worth has yet to be fully disclosed.

The word "beautiful" does not do justice to the splendors of Gyeongju. The spectacular view offered from the city as the deep orange light of the setting sun shines down on the smoothly curved ridgelines of the royal burial mounds is something that you cannot find anywhere else in the world. Gyeongju is all the more beautiful because it houses bountiful historical, natural and cultural assets. Over the ages, two thousand years of civilization were preserved with diligent care at Gyeongju, which is why the city has been designated as a World Cultural Heritage site, ensuring its continued protection in the years to come.

The spectacular view of the setting sun's rays shining down on the smoothly curved ridgelines of huge royal burial mounds is something that you cannot find anywhere but in Gyeongju.

Cheonmachong, the inside of which is open to the public, the imitations of the uncovered artifacts are placed in the positions in which they were found, and excavated relics are also displayed.

Anapji, through which one can catch a glimpse of the prosperity of the Silla kingdom, was built in the 14th year of King Munmu (674), shortly after Silla unified the Three Kingdoms. It has three central islands, and to the north and east are 12 hills, a composition reflecting East Asia's Sinseon Taoist philosophy. A number of pavilions constructed around the pond were used for state festivals and banquets in the past.

Cheomseongdae, believed to be used as an astronomical observatory during the Silla period, is the most peculiar shaped of all the relics of Gyeongju. It is a cylindrical, bottle-shaped tower on a square base, with the Chinese character 井 (jeong)-shaped stone structure at its top. This 井 (jeong)-shaped top points precisely in the directions of north, south, east and west.

Massive stone pagoda at Bunhwang Temple (**right**). This pagoda is called "Seokjeon Pagoda" because it was made of stones cut to look like bricks. Tourists holding a lotus lantern and a candle are practicing tapdori, or circling the pagoda while praying (**top**). The Silla Cultural Center plays host to topdori every weekend as part of efforts to introduce the history of the Silla kingdom to the public.

Gameunsaji 3-story stone pagoda (**right and top**). King Munmu began construction of Gameun Temple, at the foot of Mt. Yongdang, to strengthen national defense. His son, King Sinmun, completed it in 682. King Munmu willed that he be cremated and buried under a large rock off the east shore after his death so that he could become a sea dragon to protect Silla from the Japanese. The rock is now called Daewangam Rock. The underwater tomb of King Mumu (**right**).

Bulguksa, literally "Buddha Land," is a symbol of hoguk pulgyo, or state-protection Buddhism, aimed at defeating foreign invaders with the aid of Buddha. Seokga and Dabo Pagodas are both made of cut granite (**right and top**). Bulguksa, which provides an excellent example of architecture from the Silla kingdom, is a sacred place of Buddhism. The religion's deep and profound truth can be found any place at this temple.

Seokguram (**far right**) is one of the finest masterpieces from the Unified Silla kingdom. It is in complete harmony between Buddhist faith and advanced architectural skills of the time, and is also representative of Korea's traditional Buddhist art. Combined with Buddhism, the works of art by the Silla people became more exquisite and decorative, ultimately giving birth to global masterpieces such as Bulguksa and Seokguram. Beomjong (**below**), or temple bell, is rung to comfort suffering spirits in the afterlife. Honggo drum (**right**) is beat for animals and beasts.

福田函

Mt. Nam (494 m), or Namsan, is located to the south of Gyeongju. The mountain has been designated as a historical site and is referred to as an "open-field museum" because of its plethora of historic remains, including Najeong, a legendary well featured in Silla's foundation myth, and Poseokjeong, a favorite merry-making place of Silla royalty that witnessed the downfall of the kingdom. Sukgayeorae (**above**), a seated Yeorae image in Jangchangol (**left and below**), a sculpture of Buddha in a stone niche called gamsil (**left and above**).

Sinseonam Maebul (**far left**), a sitting image of a bodhisattva carved in relief on a large rock wall of a precipitous cliff. It looks as if the bodhisattva was descending on a cloud as it sits on the mountaintop, its posture peaceful and comfortable. Some 100 temples or temple ruins, 80-odd Buddhist statues or carvings and roughly 60 pagodas, including Poseokjeong (**far below**), Seochulji Pond (**below**) and Namsan's three-story stone pagoda (**left**), remain intact today.

The stone relief Buddha triad of Chilburam, "Seven Buddhas Hermitage" (**below**). The images are believed to have been carved in the early 8th century during the Unified Silla period. All four sides of one huge bolder are carved, and behind this is the Buddha triad. A sedentary statue of Amitayeorae, "Buddha of the Western Bureland" (**far below**).

Maaeyeorae Sedentary Statue, witness to 1,000 years of Silla history, today stands high overlooking Gyeongju.

Silla people's life, Silla clay figures

Ancient Silla clay figures capture what people who lived in Silla looked like over a thousand years ago in minute detail. It is said that restoring innumerable numbers of historical relics, including earthenware kilns of the Silla period, requires a deep understanding and affection for the era, as well as technical skills to produce exact replicas of the relics (**above**). Horse-mounted man-shaped earthenware pottery (**right**).

Covered with brilliant rape flowers that begin to blossom in early spring, Yongmeori, or Dragon Head Beach, stands at the foot of Mt. Sanbang. The gateway to Northeast Asia, Jeju Island has been designated the "Island of World Peace" by the Korean government.

Jeju, the Island of Many Blessings

Located off the southern tip of the Korean peninsula, Jeju Island is the nation's foremost tourist attraction. With a total area of 1,847 km^2, Jeju has a mild oceanic climate throughout the year thanks to the warm current coming up from the South China Sea. The average temperature during the hottest summer months is 33.5℃, while in the winter the barometer does not usually drop below 1.0 ℃.

The island of Jeju was formed 700,000-1.2 million years ago when lava spewed from a sub-sea volcano and emerged above the water. Then, some time between 100,000-300,000 years ago, another volcanic eruption formed Mt. Halla, which today stands in the middle of Jeju. Lava from such volcanic eruptions eventually covered the entire island.

Once called Samdado (the island of "three things in abundance") because of its abundance of rocks, wind and women, Jeju has developed remarkably since the 1960s, due in no small part to its blessed natural beauty, and has now become one of the world's great tourist paradises.

Designated as the "Island of World Peace" by the Korean government in January 2005 for its role as a place of peace and reconciliation, Jeju has grown used to being in the international spotlight. Since 1991, Mikhail Gorbachev, former President of the Soviet Union, as well as world leaders including U.S. President Bill Clinton, Japanese Prime Minister Junichiro Koizumi and Chinese President Jiang Zemin have held summit meetings on Jeju. In 2000, the island hosted the historic inter-Korean dialogue meeting between the two Koreas, cementing Jeju's role as the diplomatic center of peace and reconciliation for Northeast Asia.

According to legend, three god-men, Goh Eulna, Yang Eulna and Bu Eulna, sprang out of Samseong Shrine. These god-men married three princesses from the Byeokrang kingdom, and brought with them five types of grain seeds, calves and ponies. It is said that they founded the Tamna

kingdom, which ruled over the island from that time forward. Today, many Jeju islanders still have the last names Goh, Yang and Bu, and memorial services continue to be held at Samseong Shrine three times a year.

Dolhareubang ("Stone Grandfathers"), one of the most prominent symbols of Jeju Island, are made from porous black lava rocks. It is still not known when the first dolharubang were made, but archeologists say that these large phallic statues are similar to those found on Easter Island, Okinawa, Fiji and Bali. These statues, which range in size from 1.3 meters to 1.8 meters in height, represented gods that offered both protection and fertility, and were traditionally placed outside village entrances to protect against evil spirits while inviting good fortune. There are forty dolharubang still left on Jeju Island today.

Jeju is also home to the world's longest lava tunnel, Manjang Cave. A lava tunnel is formed when the lava that was deep in the ground spouts from the peak and flows to the surface. Manjang Cave contains many interesting features, the Stone Turtle being the most eye-catching one because it is shaped like the island of Jeju. Only 1 km of the 13.422-kilometer Manjang Cave is open to tourists.

Mt. Halla is the great divide between north and south on the island. The northern half of the island is where traditional culture is still alive and well, while the southern half is where tourism has flourished. Lying on the southern slopes of Mt. Halla is Seogwipo, the southernmost city in Korea, which is lined with many charming palm trees. Plains line the coast, and streams originating in the mountains run south to the sea, forming deep valleys and waterfalls.

In Seogwipo, Jungmun Resort Complex is a very popular tourist attraction. Among the many things people can enjoy there is Cheonjeyeon Waterfall, whose name comes from the long ago legend that the emperor of heaven's nymphs used to descend there at night to bathe in the pond at the base of this waterfall. Cheonjeyeon Waterfall is all the more beautiful because it falls between thick subtropical plants.

Yeomiji is a world-class botanical garden that provides visitors with the romance of the tropics. The 112,499 m^2 greenhouse displays over 2,000 kinds of plants and trees, and outside of this greenhouse are 1,700 varieties of trees and flowering plants all year round.

Also at Jungmun Resort Complex is Jungmun Beach, which is walled at the back by rock cliffs. Sandy hills and places for horse riding surround this beach, making the area very romantic, which is why Jungmun Beach is often used as a location for movies and TV shows.

Two kilometers west of Seogwipo is Woedolgoe ("Lonesome Rock"), named for the fact that it stands all alone at sea. This 20-meter high rock was formed during a volcanic eruption about 1.5 million years ago and makes for a fantastic scene with Beom Islet in the background. Also, Seoqwipo Port, located near the entrance of Cheonjeyeon Waterfall, offers people the chance to take a boat trip and enjoy views both over and under the water.

Mt. Halla, the highest peak in South Korea, is a splendid volcanic cone that attracts some three million tourists every year. Designated as a National Park in 1970, this shield-shaped mountain rises in the middle of Jeju Island. According to some records, the mountain erupted twice during the Goryeo dynasty, in the early 11th century. Over the years, more than 100 eruptions formed parasitic cones, or secondary volcanoes, called oreum in Jeju dialect. Today, 368 oreum are scattered all over Jeju, with Mt. Halla at the center.

Mt. Halla has long been regarded as a divine mountain where the gods reside, and is believed to protect the nation against big storms blowing in from the South Pacific. For such reasons, there are many interesting stories connected with this mountain, one being the fact that it is also called Mt. Yeongju, as it is believed that mountain gods and spirits have resided there for time immemorial. Legend also has it that spirit guardians who descended from heaven on deer played at Baeknokdam, a summit crater lake at the top of Mt. Halla.

Jeju was once a land of suffering, a place of exile for those who were expelled from the royal court. Historically, Jeju Island also served as a shield against Japanese invaders coming from the south, but recently the island has been reborn as a world-class tourist destination with breathtaking landscapes. There can be little doubt that Jeju truly is the "Island of Many Blessings."

The pristine base area around Mt. Sanbang

Legend has it that that Mt. Sanbang was borne from the peak of Mt. Halla, and that the hollow portion at the top became Baeknokdam Lake. Mt. Sangbang is said to be so beautiful that visitors cannot take their eyes off it.

Yongduam, or Dragon Head Rock (right), formed from hardened lava
The legend surrounding this unusual rock formation has it that an envoy of the Dragon King, which had been sent to Mt. Halla to bring back the elixir of eternal youth, was turned into stone by the angry mountain spirit as it tried to flee, leaving only a rocky head.

According to local legend, Cheonjeyeon Waterfall is where nymphs of the heaven's emperor used to descend at night to bathe (**top**).
Jeongbang Waterfall falls directly into the sea (**above**).
Jusangjeolli, where rocks are shaped like cubes or hexagons of various sizes that stand like handmade artifacts, as if a stonemason, and not nature, shaved and trimmed them (**right**).

Woedolgoe ("Lonesome Rock") (**left**) was sculpted from wind and wave erosion. This impressive rock appears to stand up against the might of the sea all by itself.

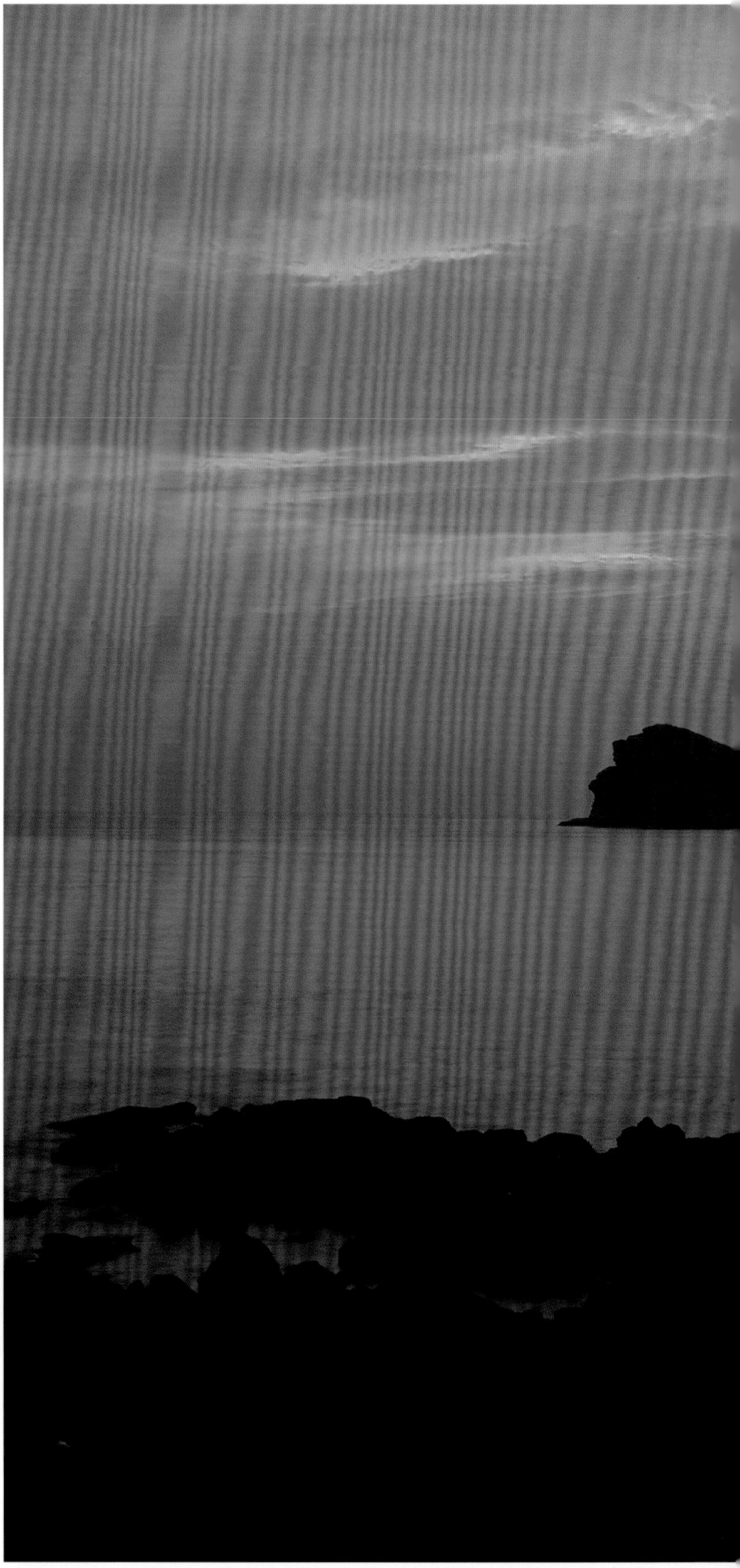

Odd shaped rocks are scattered all around Jeju, which was formed by volcanic eruptions.
Sunset on Chagwido Island ("Island of No Return") (**right**),
Sunrise on Hyeongje ("Brothers") Island (**top**),
Seongsanilchul Peak (**above middle**),
and a beach on Biyang Island ("Island that Flew to Us") (**above**).

About four kilometers off Seongsanpo is Udo, an island that is "the last home to women divers," called haenyeo in Korean, and referring to those who are born, grow up and die near the sea. Their lives revolve around the water where they harvest abalone, clams and other shellfish. These women divers, hardened by the wind and waves, it is said, dive to the ocean floor without any artificial breathing aides. About 400 - 500 haenyeo still live on Udo.

Jeju is traditionally famous for samda (three things in abundance) and sammu (three things in absence). Samda refers to the abundance of rocks, wind and women, while sammu refers to the absence of thieves, gates and beggars.

A thatch-roof house without any gates (**above**). Whereas most Korean homes used to have imposing gates to scare off would-be thieves, Jeju has historically been so safe that islanders often only leave a long log at the entrance of the house to let others know they are not home.

Jeju samulnori, samul meaning "four objects," and nori meaning "to play"(**top**).

With a subtropical climate, Jeju produces mandarin oranges and sweet pineapples (**right**).

Pyoseon Folk Village

The unique lifestyle and traditional culture of Jeju Island are presented as they appeared during the 19th century here, allowing visitors the unique opportunity to experience what life was like for Jeju islanders firsthand.

Korean fir forest and Gosamok ("the dead trees") at the top of Mt. Halla (**above**).
Baeknokdam ("White Deer Lake") is the crater lake located at the summit of Mt. Halla (**below right and above**)
Wild roe deer, one of Jeju's many tourist attractions (**top**).

Rising high in the middle of Jeju, Mt. Halla is the main symbol of the island. Mt. Halla was so named as it was thought high enough to pull at the galaxy. This 1,950-meter mountain is one of the nation's most famous mountains because of its scenic beauty. The southern part of the mountain is very steep, contrasting with the northern part, which is comparatively easier to climb. While it has four distinct seasons, it is sometimes possible to see vestiges of spring, summer, fall and winter all in one day.

Looking down from Baeknokdam Lake at sunset, the clouds colored by a setting sun make a spectacular scene.

Akjang ("musical scores"), *ilmoo* ("dance performance") and *jongmyojeryeak* ("music for religious ceremonies") are simultaneously performed during the annual Jongmyojerye Royal Ancestral Rites ceremony. Thirteen traditional Korean musical instruments are played for this ritual.

Korean Culture Stems from a Long, Vibrant History

According to *Samguksagi* ("History of the Three Kingdoms"), Korea was founded circa 2000 B.C., around the same time that the Bronze Age began on the Korean peninsula, indicating that Korean people are closely related to Bronze Age culture. Although history books point to Korean history going back only about 4,000 years, physical evidence shows that humans first began to live on the Korean peninsula in the Paleolithic Age, more than 200,000 years ago.

At the prehistoric remains site in the village of Jeongok, Yeoncheon County, daily stone tools used by primitive humans from the Lower Paleolithic Age (1 million B.C.-150,000 B.C.) to the Upper Paleolithic Age (30,000 B.C.-5,000 B.C.) have been excavated, such as bifacial hand axes and choppers. This excavation attracted keen interest from archeologists because up until these findings conventional thought had it that humans living on the Korean peninsula during the Lower Paleolithic Age were not using bifacial hand axes. It is now believed that the stone tools found at Jeongok were used as early as 200,000 B.C.

Early settlers arrived on the peninsula from the north, which is connected to the Asian continent. People of both the Paleolithic Age and the early Neolithic Age were originally hunters who lived on fish and meat. In the late Neolithic Age, however, a new group of people with a distinct culture migrated to the peninsula from the north. These were the Tungus, a largely agrarian people, who arrived around 1,000 B.C. In addition to introducing new farming techniques, they brought with them new weapons and vessels that were made of bronze, conquering or living together with the habitants who had settled on the peninsula before them, and opening the Bronze Age (1,000 B.C.-300 B.C.) in the process. Most of these Tungus were from the Ye Maek tribe, the early ancestors of today's Koreans. Culturally, this period is characterized by the birth of dolmens, the manufacturing of bronze daggers, mirrors and other bronze vessels, and the appearance of new kinds of pottery.

Goguryeo (37 B.C.-668 A.D.) subjugated neighboring tribal groups. It conquered Nakrang in 313 A.D., thereby expanding its power as far west as modern-day Liaodong, China, and began to be influenced by Huabei culture. This influence helped people living in Goguryeo create art which showed the most dynamic and buoyant rhythms of lines among the three kingdoms. These characteristics were well expressed in the mural paintings of Goguryeo tombs which have been excavated along the Yalu River in Jianl and Tonggou, as well as around Pyeongyang and Anak, Hwanghae province.

Baekje (18-660) was located in the western coastal area,

south of the Han River, where the climate was relatively mild. This region did not have any high or rugged mountains, and instead contained many low, gently sloping ones. The art of Baekje reflected such natural aspects, with very gentle and smooth lines. The peaceful serenity of the area, like that of Buddha's smile, for example, is found in many Baekje artworks, a kingdom which represented the very smooth curves of early Korean art.

Silla (57 B.C.-935 A.D.) was founded in Gyeongju, which is located in the southeastern coastal region of the peninsula. This kingdom showed the finest, most glorious form of art among the three kingdoms. The unique art of Silla later became influenced by other cultures, as more splendid colors and ornaments were added after Silla allied itself with the Tang dynasty of China and conquered both Baekje and Goguryeo, unifying the three kingdoms. The Silla of the Three Kingdoms Period before unification is referred to as "Old Silla," while the kingdom after unification is called "Unified Silla" (or Tongil Silla).

Although many chiefdoms and kingdoms rose and fell on the Korean peninsula up until the time of the Goryeo dynasty (918-1392), they largely had cultural exchanges with China only. Monks of the three kingdoms had religious exchanges with India, but it was the Goryeo dynasty that first began to hold political, economic and cultural exchanges with other nations.

With the fall of Silla, art was taken over by Goryeo and went into decline. The Goryeo dynasty, after overcoming early social disorder and gaining stability, began to inspire the vigorous spirit of the north into its overall culture, blending the characteristics of Goryeo and Silla art, which was falling into decay at the time. Goryeo made Buddhism the state religion and put powerful Buddhist policies into action. It encouraged the publishing of many Buddhist scriptures, leading to the development of printing technology. It was the Goryeo dynasty, in fact, that invented the world's first movable metal printing type in 1234, replacing wood carving and wooden movable type. Korea's *Jikji Simche Yojeol* ("Anthology of the Great Buddhist Monks' Zen Teachings") was officially recognized by UNESCO as the oldest known book of movable metal print in the world. Also, the world's oldest publication made from woodblock printing, the *Dharani Sutra*, which was printed in 751, was discovered at Bulguksa's Seokga Pagoda in 1966.

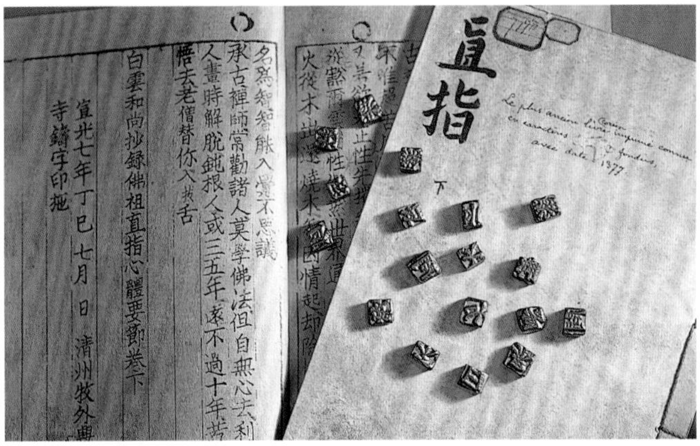

The people of the Goryeo dynasty showed a deep religious devotion by carving Buddhist sutras onto wooden printing blocks. At the national level, they carved the *Tripitaka Koreana*, or Buddhist Canon, onto roughly 80,000 wooden printing blocks to protect the kingdom from foreign enemies. The *Tripitaka Koreana*, designated as a World Heritage cultural relic by UNESCO, is now stored at Haeinsa, a temple in Hapcheon, South Gyeongsang province.

The Joseon dynasty (1392-1910) was founded by Lee Seong-gye, the ambitious great general of Goryeo. Blaming the fall of Goryeo on the depravity of Buddhism, the Joseon dynasty adopted policies to drive out Buddism, while enthusiastically introducing Confucianism, which put an emphasis on morality. At the same time, the Joseon dynasty implemented a "Northern Policy" that, instead of aiming to regain the old territory of Goguryeo, was neither ambitious nor imperialistic. This nonchalant and carefree attitude was also reflected in the art, leading to the creation of unique paintings and Joseon baekja (white porcelain). Ultimately, it was Hangeul, the written form of Korean, invented by King Sejong in the 15th century, however, that represented the most remarkable progress in Joseon culture, and not porcelain.

Nestled along the Nakdong River sits Andong Hahoe village

This folk village maintains the same traditional culture that has been passed down for hundreds of years. In particular, Hahoe Byeolsingut Mask Dance, a form of mask drama presented by performers wearing hahoe masks, is regarded as the top Korean mask dance, showing the corrupt side of Buddhism by satirizing a monk who was seduced by a flirtatious young woman called Bune long ago.

Sarcastic Hahoe Mask Dance

This mask dance is essentially a satire on moral attitudes and social classes. *Hahoe* masks are conspicuously different from other Korean masks in that they are all incredibly realistic in appearance. Although only a few thick lines form the face, they express the unique personality of each character brilliantly.

Cheoyongmu (Dance of Cheoyong)
Cheoyongmu is also called Obangmu, or a dance performed in five directions. The *cheoyong* mask, the symbol of Ulsan, South Gyeongsang province, is a familiar bearded face with a gentle smile. The peony put on the head represents wealth, while the spray represents the act of expelling evil spirits. The mask is made based on the image of Cheoyong as described in *Akhakgwebeom,* a story written during the reign of King Seongjong (1469-1494).

Salpuri ("Scarf Dance") was developed from a shamanistic rite in which a living person talks with the spirit of a dead person through a psychic medium (**right**). *Haegeum* is a stringed instrument played by rubbing a bow between two strings (**right and center**). *Daegeum*, or a large bamboo flute, produces a distinctive buzzing sound that is both refined and solemn (**far right**).

Seong Chang-sun, who has been designated a Human Cultural Asset by the Korean government, says that singers can gain a perfect voice if they practice hard to produce sounds that are louder than the sound of a waterfall (**right and below**).
Hwaguanmu ("Flower Dance") used to be performed to entertain the king or upper class citizens (**far below**).
Taepyeongmu ("Dance of Peace") was performed to pray for the peaceful reign of the king and for a bountiful harvest (**below**).

Buchaechum ("Fan Dance")

Widely regarded as the most unique Korean traditional dance, *buchaechum* shows the beauty of vivid colors and the harmony of group movements in a set space. This splendid dance is performed mainly by spreading, folding and turning fans, and in this process induces the dancers to move their whole bodies. *Buchaechum* illustrates the sublime harmony of both dynamic and static movements.

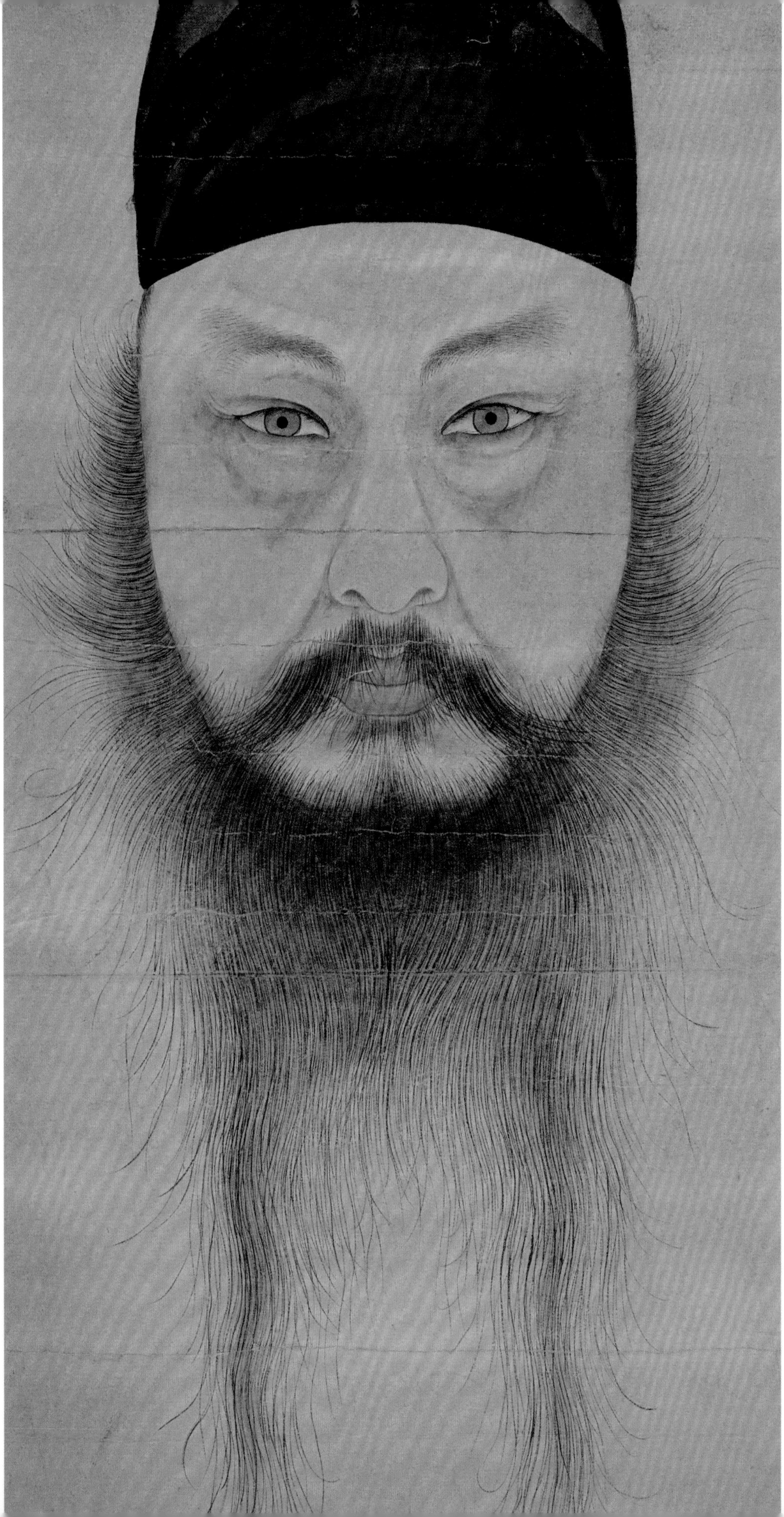

Self-portrait of Yun Du-seo, a Scholar-artist of the Late Joseon Dynasty

By concentrating only on the facial area, this unique portrait captures a heightened sense of self-awareness. The realistic description of his sharp eyes, moustache and beard is unprecedented, making this painting one of the best preserved portraits from the Joseon dynasty.

Genre Paintings of the Late Joseon Dynasty

"Lovers under the Moonlight," (**above**) is one of painter Shin Yun-bok's best known works, the man who is widely regarded as one of the greatest genre painting artists from this period. "Boy Playing a Flute" (**left**) was painted by Kim Hong-do, who rivaled Shin Yun-bok as one of the greatest artists in genre painting. "The Scholar Enjoying Leisure Time between Readings" (**right**) by Jeong Seon is the realistic portrayal of a scholar who leisurely spends his time.

Celadon Incense Burner Topped by Kylin, a Mythical Creature

Celadon Kettle in the Shape of a Flying Dragon

Celadon Kettle in the Shape of a Turtle

White Porcelain Water Dropper with Embossed Crane Pair Design

White Octagonal-shaped Porcelain Water Dropper with Landscape Design

White Porcelain Jar with Iron-painted Plum and Bamboo Design (right)
This well-rounded white porcelain jar displays unrivalled beauty in shape, color and painting skill. It is evenly glazed in a bluish white color. Mastering the skill of painting plum and bamboo suggests that it was the work of a prominent court painter.

Artisan Sticking to the Traditional Pottery-making Methods
Artisan Cheon Han-bong creates a pot by using a foot-powered spinning wheel, a method handed down over many generations. He says that glazing and firing techniques determine the quality and characteristics of pottery. *Maksabal*, literally "rough bowls," were used by the common people during the Joseon dynasty.

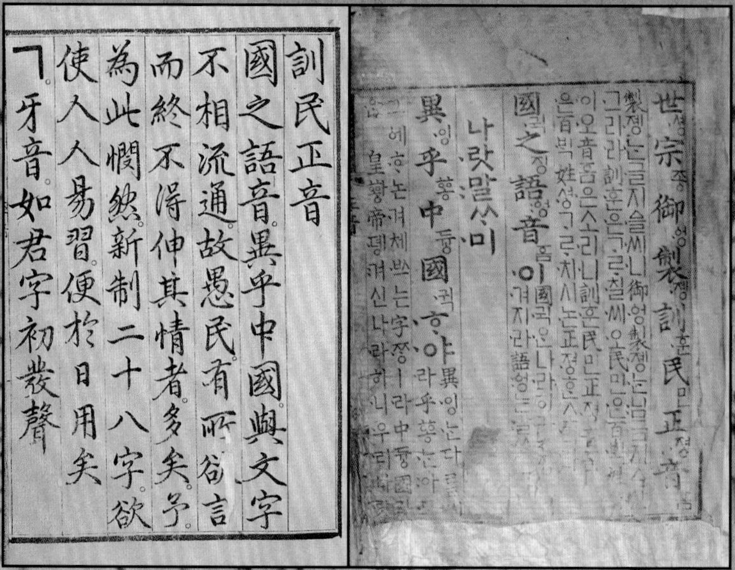

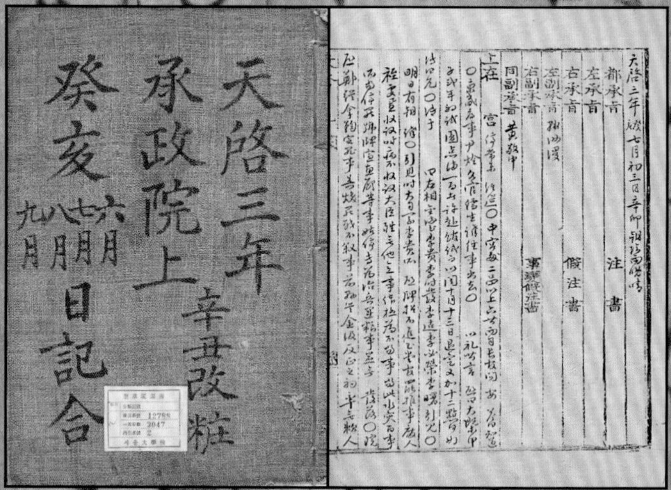

Jikji simche yojeol (Anthology of the Great Buddhist Monks' Zen Teachings), the world's oldest known book of movable metal print (**above**)
Hunminjeongeum, literally "the Correct Sounds for the Instruction of the People" (**right and above**), *Seungjeongwonilgi*, (the daily records of the royal secretariat during the Joseon dynasty) (**right and center**)
Joseonwangjosilrok, a collection of historical records from the Joseon dynasty (**right and below**)
These four are all designated as World Documentary Heritage items.

Creation of *Hunminjeongeum*, the Nation's Greatest Cultural Heritage Legacy

Koreans were using Chinese characters before *Hunminjeongeum* was invented. Hangeul (the Korean alphabet) was created by King Sejong and scholars from the Jiphyeonjeon, an academic research institute of the Joseon dynasty.

***Tripitaka Koreana* (a Buddhist Canon)**

Carved onto roughly 80,000 wooden printing blocks, *Tripitaka Koreana* is said to have been made with the help of Buddha to protect Korea from foreign invaders. An aerial view of Janggyeonggak (**right**) at Haein Temple, where the *Tripitaka Koreana* wooden printing blocks are stored (**above**).

Windows used to be latticed, with the lower portions being made three times bigger than the upper portions in an effort to control humidity inside Janggyeonggak. This is a very scientific ventilation method that shows the wisdom of past architects and engineers (**left**).

Suwon Fortress

Suwon Hwaseong, or Suwon Fortress, was built in the late Joseon dynasty by King Jeongjo in an attempt to display filial piety toward his father. It was constructed under the direction of Jeong Yak-yong, a young scholar who would later go on to lead institutional reform and practical application of academic theories. The fortress wall was built according to unprecedented scientific principles, making Suwon Fortress the epitome of Korea's fortification construction knowledge and techniques.

Also known as Gochangeup Fortress, this castle was built to protect Korea from the Japanese. The tradition of treading on the fortress walls originates in the legend that one round will relieve you of any leg pains; two rounds will give you a long and healthy life; and three rounds will guarantee you a place in heaven after death.

Dolmens, Stone Graves of the Bronze Age

These dolmens date back to about 5,000 B.C.-3,000 B.C., when humans were using bronze tools. There are about 70,000 dolmens around the world, over 30,000 scattered in Korea alone. The group of dolmens in Ganghwa Island, Gochang County and Hwasun County are inscribed on UNESCO's World Cultural Heritage list.

서울역
광화문
시청

Taekwondo, the Spirit of Korea

Officially recognized as an Olympic sport, taekwondo is not just a martial art. Taekwondo is steeped in a long history that involves a respect of human dignity, self-control over body and mind, and self-realization, values that all represent the spirit of Korea. Taekwondo also teaches children proper manners, integrity, cooperation, fellowship and leadership.

Taekwondo as a Whole-body Sport

All nine marble boards break into pieces with just one strike of the hand, while all the boards are instantly smashed with just one mighty kick. Taekwondo is a whole-body sport, making use of the arms and legs in particular. It is not only a martial art for self-defense, but also a means of cultivating one's personality through the training of body and mind.

Dodamsam ("Three Rocks") Peak
The most famous of Danyang's eight great attractions, Dodamsam Peak has a heavenly serenity to it, especially when shrouded by early morning mist.

Sublime Scenery that Holds the Mystery of Nature

Surrounded by water on three sides, Korea enjoys the natural beauties of both land and sea. The nation is located in the temperate zones of the Northern Hemisphere and has four distinct seasons. In spring, various wild flowers and verdurous trees cover the mountains. When summer arrives, leaves turn a deep green, and the crystal clear water running through the many valleys of the country becomes cold enough to reduce the scorching heat. As autumn deepens, leaves change from green to red and gold, culminating in an awe-inspiring beauty.

The snow-covered winter landscape is the epitome of the country's natural scenic beauty. The mountains and rivers are so uniquely serene that they are reminiscent of many Oriental ink paintings. From time immemorial Korea has been called geumsugangsan, which means "mountains and rivers as beautiful as if they were embroidered on silk." Korea's national parks are particularly picturesque in this regard.

The Korean peninsula has a vast number of magnificent mountain ranges which branch out from the Baekdu Mountain Range, the Taebaek Mountain Range forming the backbone of the peninsula. Situated north of the Taebaek Mountain Range, Mt. Seorak National Park attracts mountain climbers all year round with its superb scenic beauty that changes every season. Mt. Seorak leads up to the Gaema Plateau in North Korea via Mt. Geumgang, and runs down south to the Charyeong and Sobaek Mountain Ranges. The highest peak in the Taebaek Mountain Range, Mt. Seorak stands 1,708 meters above sea level. The whole mountain is literally a huge block of rock, just as its name in Korean implies, that was formed when it started to split and break, its cracks eventually becoming valleys connected in a ridgeline. Mt. Seorak is divided into two parts: Oeseorak and Naeseorak, or Outer Seorak and Inner Seorak. Outer Seorak is closest to the sea and Inner Seorak is farther inland.

Mt. Seorak displays a totally different landscape depending on the season. When spring comes, its slopes become a cornucopia of various shades of pink, purple and white, with the flowering of azaleas and rhododendrons. In summer, clouds and fog veil the peaks, creating "the islands of peculiar-shaped rocks" that seem to rise above the waves of clouds, the valleys appearing to suddenly vanish in the sea of fog. When a full moon comes out in the dark autumn sky, the rocky peaks look like dancing nymphs from heaven. In winter, the mountain is blanketed white from its peaks to its cliffs and streams. Snow that covers tree branches forms full-blown flowers.

In the southern part of the Korean peninsula soars Mt. Jiri. Designated as the nation's first national park in 1967, Mt. Jiri also occupies the largest total land area for a park (440.485 km^2), straddling the borders of three provinces, South Jeolla province, North Jeolla province and South Gyeongsang province.

Mt. Jiri has long been referred to as one of the Samsinsan ("Three Gods Mountains"), along with Mt. Geumgangn and Mt. Halla. In days of old, it was the Namak ("Southern Mountain") of the five mountains that surrounded Silla, and was given the name Mt. Jiri because of the wisdom that was bestowed on anyone who stayed there. The mountain is also home to several famous Buddhist temples, such as Hwaeomsa, Yeongoksa, Daewonsa and Silsangsa. Collectively, the temples store many precious Buddhist cultural properties.

The many different aspects of nature that can be seen at Mt. Jiri are nothing short of spectacular. There are times when an endless sea of thick clouds covers the entire mountain, only to suddenly change into a hazy fog. At other times a deep blue sky hangs above the lush green forest, fields and valleys. The numerous mountain ridges create a sense of majestic waves washing over the mountain, and the virgin forest and crystal clear water produce an unrivaled pure natural beauty.

One of the country's many national parks, Dado Maritime National Park is made up of over 1,700 islands, and is located in the southern part of the peninsula. It features a breathtaking mix of peculiar-shaped islands, emerald skies, rich cobalt sea, and endless white sandy beaches that are fringed with thick pine forests. In fact, the national park gives off a different appearance every minute of the day. In the morning, the landscape looks as if it has emerged from a traditional Korean ink painting; at midday it changes into a figurative Western painting with a realistic description of many distinct looking rocks; and when the sun goes down, the magical red-colored scenery becomes similar to an impressionist painting.

Designated as a natural monument for its protection, Hongdo ("Red Island") is an ecological treasure house, the natural habitat of many rare plants and animals. The entire shore of the island is decorated either with reddish brown rocks or steep cliffs, which have been carved over time by the forces of erosion. With a total area of only 6.87 square kilometers, Hong Island enchants tourists with its curious-looking rocks scattered along the beach, such as Dolphin Rock, Rainbow Rock and Pillar Rock.

The nation's third biggest island, consisting of 42 inhabited and 189 uninhabited islets, Jin Island is famous for "Moses' Miracle." The event takes its name from the fact that early every March a dry road suddenly appears in the middle of the sea, resembling what happened in the Old Testament's Book of Exodus. Tens of thousands of tourists flock to Jin Island annually to enjoy this marvelous sight.

Nestled on Geoje Island in Hallyeo Maritime National Park is Oedo Maritime Botanical Garden, appropriately called the "Paradise of the South." This tourist attraction is replete with exotic subtropical plants and trees, as well as an indigo colored sea background. Its beauty is the perfect compliment to nearby Haegeumgang Island, the "Mt. Geumgang of the South Sea." almost 30 years to cultivate what is.

About a seven-hour boat ride from Yeosu sits an uninhabited place called Baek Island. The mystical island and its rocks, which resemble statues created by a skilled artist, are constantly veiled by thick sea fog under an oddly clear sky. Legend has it that the son of heaven's emperor was sent to the island because the emperor was angry with him. The son fell in love with the daughter of the dragon god, and ended up enjoying his time there. After many years, the emperor yearned to see his son, so sent ninety-eight subjects to retrieve him. The son, however, refused to come back. Furious, the emperor then turned his son and the subjects into rocks. These rocks now form what is Baek Island, which stands guard in the middle of the sea here as if it and its surrounding rocks have been plucked from a work of art.

This tourist attraction, which took almost 30 years to cultivate, is replete...

Mt. Seorak's mysteriousness enchants visitors with its smooth ridgelines, steep rocks and deep valleys (**right**). Long known as a divine mountain, Mt. Mai ("Horse Ears' Mountain") is famous for Tap Temple (**above left**). Gosamok, or dead trees, at Mt. Gyeryong highlights the mystery of nature (**far above**).

Ssangcheon Valley, Seorak-dong is covered with snow throughout the winter. In spring, melting snow flows down through the valley. In summer, the water swells and runs like a wild river. In autumn, the valley is bursting with gorgeous red and gold maple leaves.

Sparkling clean water runs down between moss-grown rocks (**right**). Korea enjoys a variety of native plants that change with the seasons. There are about 4,500 kinds of wild plants in the nation. From top to bottom, adonis amurensis, bleeding heart and Chrysanthemum zawadskii herb.

Daegwanryeong Snow Blossom Festival

A winter wonderland, Daegwanryeong Snow Blosoom Festival is held in an area famous for its clean air, deep valleys, magnificent mountains and long winter. Tourists and villagers alike revel in the romantic winter atmosphere as they make snowmen and snow sculptures.

Natural Cave, a Mystical Underground Palace
A natural cave buried deep under the Earth reveals some of the mysteries that have been created here over hundreds of millions of years. Although Korea is not a large country, it has an unrivalled number of natural caves, one of nature's greatest creations.

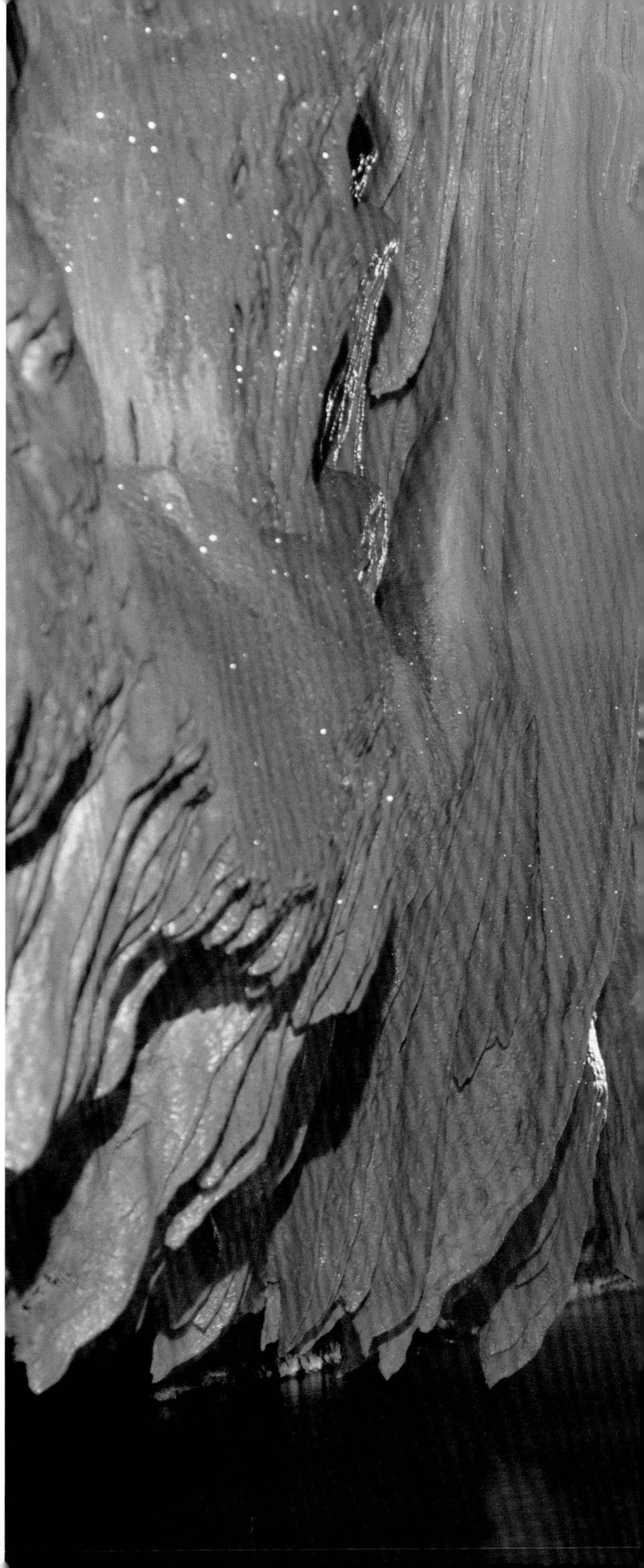

The shore of Hongdo ("Red Island") is surrounded by intriguing rocks, which take on a different hue according to the sunlight. The entire island is designated as a natural monument.

Islands with Their Own Scenic Beauty

Seonyu Island is blessed with clear skies and sea, and is noted for its magnificent view at sunset. Seonyudo means "the island where Taoist hermits play" (**left**). Surrounded by clear blue water, Somaemul Island has many captivating rocky cliffs (**below**). Twenty-eight kilometers from Geomun Island, Baek Island (**far left**) is well-known for its unique rocks, which have been shaped by erosion over time by the forces of water. The beauty of Baek Island has made it one of the major attractions of Dadohae Maritime National Park.

Part of the easternmost island group of Korea, Dokdo (**left**) is situated 90 kilometers southeast of Ulleung Island. It is a volcanic island group made up of 36 rocky islets, including the two relatively large ones of Dongdo ("East Island") and Seodo ("West Island"). One fifth of the Ulleung Island coast consists of cliffs, where various-sized sea caves and eroded rocks in the indigo colored sea create an exotic atmosphere (**far below**).

"Moses' Miracle" of Korea

As the sea waters part, a dry road emerges in the middle of the sea. This 2.8-kilometer long sea passage links Jin Island, South Jeolla province, with a smaller offshore islet called Mo Island. Referred to as "Moses' Miracle" of Korea for its similarity to the Biblical parting of the Red Sea, this phenomenon takes place four times a year, around mid-April and mid-May.

A fresh sea breeze blows into the faces of passengers on a boat (**far right and below**). People line up on the beach at sunset under a deep indigo sky (**above**). Women enjoy a midsummer day with a mudpack on their faces (**right**). The sun sets over a spectacular horizon (**far right and above**).

Adventure Sports : Traditional Activities

Many Koreans have taken to mountain biking these days, while those seeking a greater adventure enjoy paragliding in the country's clear skies. Korea's challenging rapids have also made whitewater rafting a popular sport. And rock climbing, both on mountains and out on sea rocks, has caught on lately, even among amateur climbers.

***Daljiptaeugi*, ("Burn the Straw Hut")**

Daljiptaeugi is one of the nation's folk customs performed on Daeboreum (the year's first full moon), which falls on the fifteenth day of the first month according to the lunar calendar. People turn around a burning straw hut, making wishes for the year on this occasion.

Traditional Annual Customs

Annual customs refer to cyclical rites and rituals repeatedly observed over a long period of time, and usually based on seasonal divisions, or *jeolgi* as they are known in Korean. These are often determined by an area's natural environment, local history and social groups, or a primary industry of a particular region. In Korea, annual customs have traditionally integrated a wide array of rituals, incantations, taboos, and physical activities that center around agriculture. As one of the most celebrated holidays in Korea, Seollal, Lunar New Year's Day, is a festive occasion when family members get together to pay their respects to their ancestors.

On the eve of Seollal, people clean their houses so that they can welcome the New Year on a fresh note. In the past, people used to make *seolbim*, new clothes, especially for the upcoming New Year. Such a practice still remains today, so that many Koreans dress their best for Seollal, some even wearing *hanbok* (traditional Korean dress), which is rarely worn in everyday life anymore. Dressed up in seolbim on the morning of Seollal, families gather to perform charye, an annual ritual service to pay their respects to ancestors. After *charye*, participants drink the very same tea or alcohol that was used for the service. Originally, tea was served during *charye*, the "cha" in *charye* meaning "tea" in Korean. But beginning in the Joseon dynasty, an increasing number of households replaced tea with alcoholic beverages. The main dish for *charye* is rice cake soup, *ddeokguk*. Though its exact origin is not known, *ddeokguk* has long been the most popular dish on Seollal.

After eating *ddeokguk* for breakfast, younger members of the family perform New Year's bows to their elders, who in return offer New Year's greetings and best wishes. The whole family then visits the graves of their ancestors to pay their respects and pray for a year of good fortune, which is followed by a variety of traditional games like yutnori (a four-stick board game), *neolddwigi* (Korean seesaw), *jegichagi* (shuttlecock kicking), *paengichigi* (top spinning) and *yeonnaligi* (kite flying).

The 15th day of the first month in the lunar calendar is called Daeboreum, an occasion when the festive mood that starts with Seollal reaches its peak. An auspicious day is selected around Daeboreum to perform antaek or dongje, the former is a personal ritual to wish for the family's prosperity, the latter a collective service dedicated to a village guardian deity. As soon as people get up on the appointed day, usually early in the morning, they often crack a variety of nuts, such as pine nuts, walnuts, chestnuts and peanuts, in the belief that these will make their skin and teeth healthy throughout the year. Tradition also has it that a cup of unheated alcohol, gwibalgisul, should be consumed before breakfast.

A wide variety of winter games are played from Seollal through Daeboreum, including *daljiptaeugi* (straw house burning), *jwibulnori* (swirling of fire-lit cans), *juldarigi* (tug of war), *daribalpgi* (bridge treading), *jisinbalpgi* (stepping on the spirit of the earth), and *notdaribalpgi* (crossing of a human bridge).

In Korea, Buddha's birthday is grandly celebrated. Falling on the eighth day of the fourth month according to the lunar calendar, most Buddhist temples across the nation hold special ceremonies as well as an array of cultural events on the day. Of particular note is the Lotus Lantern Festival, whose purpose it is to enlighten the secular world with the light of wisdom, while also admiring the mercy of Buddha that illuminates darkness and ignorance.

The fifth day of the fifth month on the lunar calendar is called Dano, which used to be one of the biggest holidays of the year during the Joseon dynasty, along with Seollal and Chuseok (Harvest Moon Festival). Typical dishes widely enjoyed during Dano festivities include wheat noodles and various rice cakes made of spring vegetables. On the day of Dano itself, women used to wash their hair and perform facial massages with iris water. They would also collect morning dew from iris flowers for their makeup. An extremely rare flower that blooms once every century, the iris was believed to have a unique scent that could drive away evil spirits and bad luck. Special events for Dano include *ssireum* (Korean wrestling) and *geuneddwigi* (swinging), the former is for men, the latter for women.

Chuseok, also known as Hangawi and the Harvest Moon Festival, is another major traditional holiday in Korea, celebrated on the 15th day of the eighth lunar month, when abundant crops and fruits are fully ripe in the fields. As an occasion to give thanks for the year's harvest, Chuseok is observed as enthusiastically as Seollal. During Chuseok, family members get together to celebrate the holiday. Befitting its name, Chuseok features a great number of special dishes, among which *songpyeon* is the most famous. *Songpyeon* is a rice cake in the shape of a half moon, stuffed with sesame, beans, chestnuts and dates. In light of the fact that Koreans used to observe the lunar calendar, they made these special rice cakes to express their gratitude toward the moon. People perform an ancestor worship ritual on Chuseok with *songpyeon* called *jesa*, in which all the family members are involved. Traditional activities for Chuseok include *nongak* (farmers' percussion music), *ganggangsuwollae* (a circle dance for women) and *ssireum*.

Marriage is one of the most important rites of passage in cultures throughout the world. Even ancient civilizations are known to have had their own unique marriage customs. The Korean word for marriage, "*hon*," is a homonym for "dusk," which is why a marriage ritual can also be translated as "a rite performed at dusk" in Korean. This makes perfect sense because a wedding ceremony is a perfect union of yin (female) and yang (male), and dusk is also a rendezvous point between yin (night) and yang (day). The reason why dusk is chosen over dawn, another merging point of night and day, is that the married couple needs to spend the first night together after the ceremony.

Koreans have long regarded longevity and a natural, peaceful death as one of the most blissful things that should be strived for. Ancestral worship is so ingrained in everyday life that most Koreans regard death as part of an eternal life with their offspring, not as leaving for good. Funeral rites vary depending on regional or family traditions, but most funeral services are bound to observe several proper steps. Traditionally, villagers got together to carry the coffin to the burial site as the bereaved family members following close behind. Once the service was over, the coffin could either be burned or interred in a hut built to store such items.

Public awareness of cultural heritage in Korea has been heightened even as traditional culture disappears as a result of globalization. Yet just as the value of cultural identity is highly recognized in a multicultural system, annual customs and folk games, which themselves are an epitome of traditional Korean culture, are now being brought back to the forefront of society.

A thatch-roof house is seen over the low stone fence. Covered with snow that fell overnight, the village makes visitors feel as if they've been transported back in time to the Joseon dynasty. The Korean Folk Village is reminiscent of scenery in many traditional ink paintings.

Autumn is the harvest season for farmers, and good reason to celebrate, as they have been working hard since the spring.

Good-natured People

Farmers' broad, healthy smiles reflect their good-natured and warm personalities. Living simple lives, these Korean farmers are generous and kindhearted people.

Ganggangsuwollae (circle dance for women) is a traditional Korean folk activity enjoyed by young women and girls on Chuseok (Thanksgiving Day), which falls on the fifteenth day of the eighth lunar month. Women hold hands with each other and dance around in a circle while singing. This circle dance starts very slowly and gradually gets faster, eventually accelerating to a rapid, whirling climax.

Traditional Korean Folk Games

Yutnori (a four-stick board game) is one of Korea's most popular traditional games. It is usually played on Seollal, Lunar New Year's Day (**far above**). This game is played by throwing four sticks in the air and then calculating the score according to the five combinations of the fronts and backs of the sticks. The combinations are called *do*, *gae*, *geol*, *yut* and *mo*, meaning "pig," "dog," "sheep," "cow" and "horse," respectively, and which have all been essential animals to farming in Korea for centuries. *Jegichagi* (shuttlecock kicking) is played mainly by male children with their feet (**above**). Designated as Intangible Cultural Property No. 58, *jultagi* (tightrope feat) is performed on a rope three meters high, which can make it very dangerous (**right**).

New Year's Day Customs
Early in the morning on Seollal, family members perform *charye* (memorial service for ancestors), after which they sit down to eat the same food that was used in the ceremony (**right**). Once finished with the ceremony, young family members perform sebae, or traditional New Year's bows, to their elders (**far right**).

Korean Food for Traditional Holidays

On the morning of Seollal, Koreans eat *ddeokguk* (rice cake soup) to greet the New Year (**below**). Out of an ancient belief that the year should start with solemnity and purity, pure white *ddeokguk* is served on Seollal. A whole family sits to make *songpyeon* in the shape of half moons (**left and below**). *Songpyeon* is rice cake steamed on a layer of pine needles, which keeps many different *songpyeon* from sticking to each other and also functions as protection against bacteria (**far below**). *Songpyeon* is the most common food served on Chuseok.

Kimchi, Koreans' Favorite Traditional Food

The most visible side dish in Korea, kimchi is an essential part of any Korean meal. *Bossam* kimchi, or wrap-up kimchi (**far above**), *baechu dongchimi*, or cabbage water kimchi (**above and center**), *dongchimi* (**above**), and baechu kimchi, or cabbage kimchi (**right and above**), are just some of the many varieties of different kimchi.

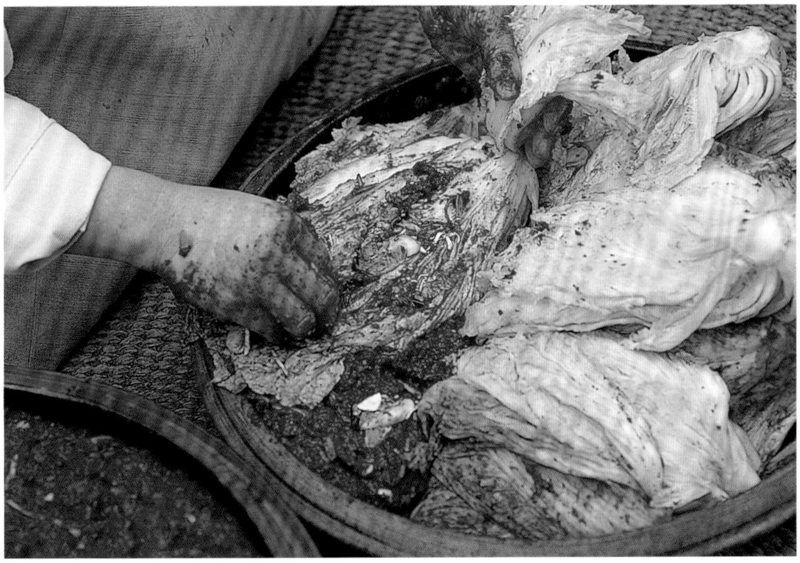

Bibimbap (Boiled Rice Mixed with Vegetables)

Samgyetang (Ginseng Chicken Soup)

Galbi (Short Ribs of Beef)

Naengmyeon (Noodles Mixed with Cold Soup)

Traditional Korean food boasts a wide range of vivid colors. When preparing food, Koreans are careful to make sure the food looks as aesthetically appealing as it is delicious.

A myriad recipes have been handed down in Korea throughout the country's 5,000 years of history, including *gujeolpan*, or nine different items on a divided wooden plate (**above**), and *dasik*, or traditional sweets (**right**). A traditional table setting (**below**) and a drinking table setting (**far right**) will often include many side dishes. On the drinking table are dried slices of fish, fish eggs, dried seafood, *jeon* (Korean pancakes), *pyeonyuk* (pressed boiled beef), *jjim* (braised meat or fish), *sinseonro*, or casserole dish (**right and above**). Kimchi, fruits, vegetables and *jeotgal* (fermented seafood) are also served on this table. **(Food prepared by Prof. Han Young-sil of Sookmyung Women's University)**

Hanbok, literally "Korean dress," is the traditional clothing that Koreans today wear for formal events. With supreme beauty in line, shape and color, hanbok displays excellent weaving and dyeing skills.

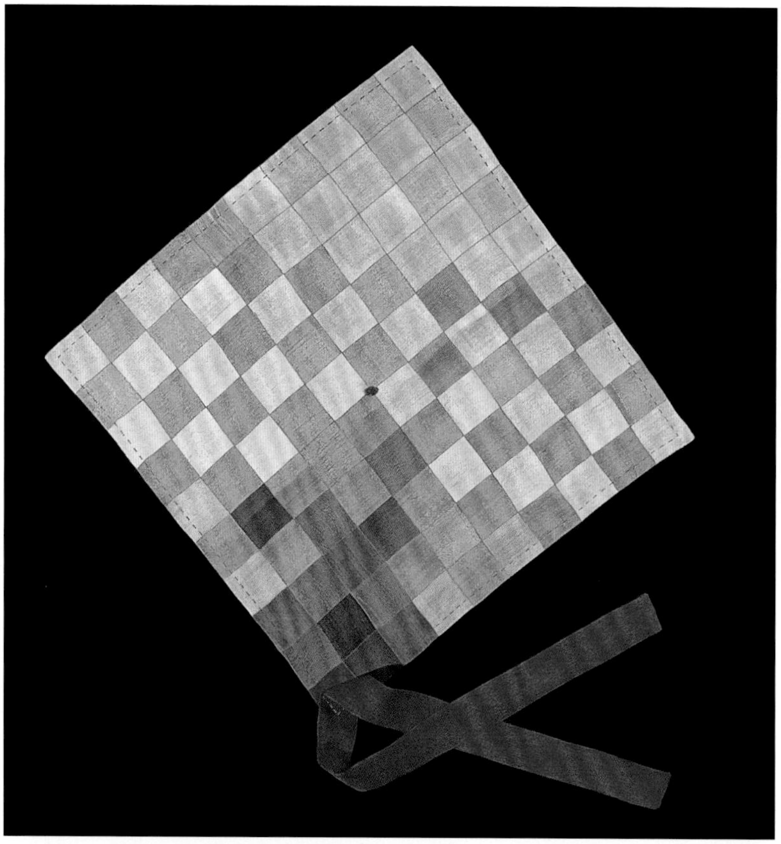

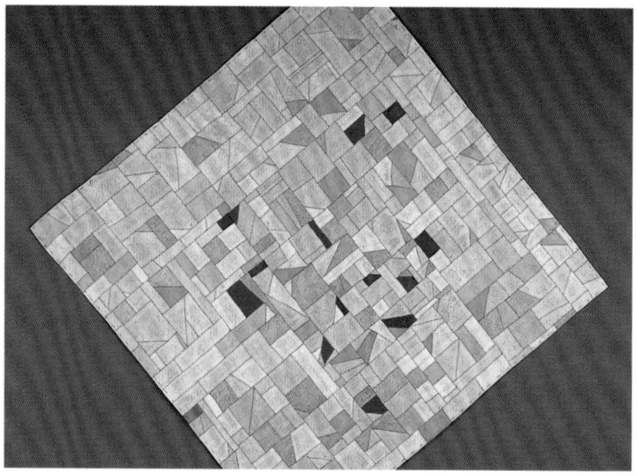

Patchwork cloths sewn together from tiny scraps of fabric show the aesthetic delicacy and wisdom of Korean women (**far left**). *Hwalot* (a noblewoman's wedding ceremonial dress) is luxuriously embroidered. The front (**above**) and the back (**below**) of *hwalot*.

Traditional Folk Rituals and Plays

Koreans believed that red-colored food would scare away evil spirits and usher in health and prosperity. Out of this belief, they placed red bean porridge on *jangdokdae* (an outdoor jar stand) and held a special ritual on Dongji, the winter solstice (**left and above**). *Jisinbalpgi* (stepping on the spirit of the earth) is a traditional folk activity in which farmers with percussion instruments go from house to house and wish people good luck (**left**). Gossaum is a kind of tug-of-war game using huge straw ropes (**far left**) that is especially popular in South Jeolla province. *Daljiptaeugi* (burning the straw hut) was performed to ward off bad spirits and pray for good luck (**above**) in the past.

Nongak (Farmers' Percussion Band Music Performance)
Nongak is a Korean folk activity when farmers, usually on traditional holidays, play their instruments and dance to brighten people's spirits (**right, right and below**), inspiring the village in turn to bring about *sinmyeong* ("people's enthusiasm"). One of the nongak band members is turning a sangmo, a hat with a long white rope (**below**).

***Samulnori,* Harmony of the Sky, Earth and Humans**

Samul refers to the four basic percussion instruments used for *nongak*. The *buk* (drum) and the *janggu* (hour-glass shaped drum), both made of leather, represent the voice of the earth, while the *kkwaenggari* (small gong) and the *jing* (large gong), both made of metal, represent the voice of the sky. These instruments combine with human voices to create a harmonized voice of the sky, earth and humans (**left**).

Salt
Salt
된장
Kim chi
고추장
Sugar

"Nanta," a Must-see Performance

While cooking, the performers turn all kinds of kitchen items into percussion instruments. Created by adopting the rhythms and beats of *samulnori*, "Nanta" has been a huge success, both in Korea and overseas.

Traditional Wedding Ritual in Korea

On a bride's wedding day, she traditionally wore a colorful ceremonial dress called a *wonsam*, while putting a bridal tiara, *jokduri*, on her head and *yeonji* and *gonji* (large red dots) on her cheeks and forehead, respectively. The groom traditionally put on a *samogwandae* (horsehair hat and decorated belt). A religious ceremony is performed to honor their ancestors and promote the bearing of children so that the family line may continue.

Traditional Funeral Rites

Among the four *gwanhonsangje* ceremonies (coming-of-age, marriage, funeral and ancestor worship), funeral services are observed most deferentially, and have undergone the fewest changes over the years. Funeral rites reflect what Koreans believe about life after death as well as filial piety.

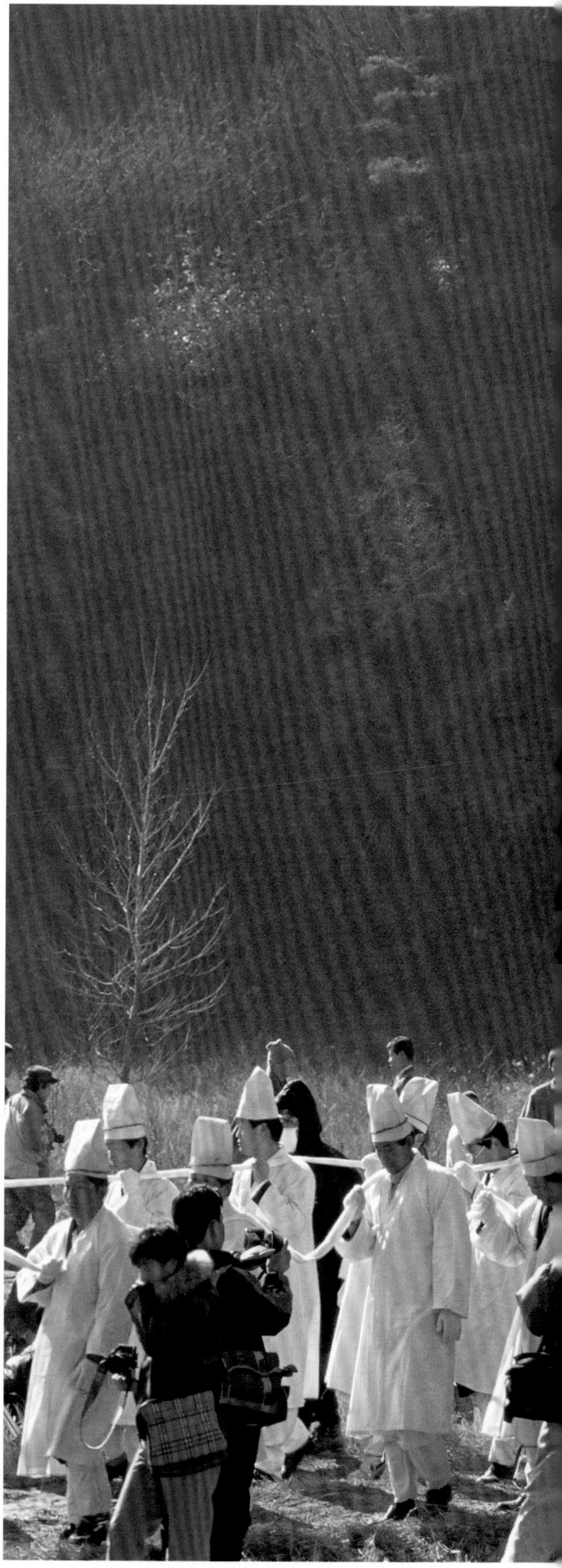

Sije (Time Rite), Memorial Service for Ancestors

Sije services are performed to honor one's ancestors. These rites nurture intergenerational bonding and pride (**left and above**). *Myoje* rites are held at gravesites in October of the lunar calendar every year. Before a *sije* service is conducted, *sansinje* is performed to worship the spirits of the mountain (**far above**).

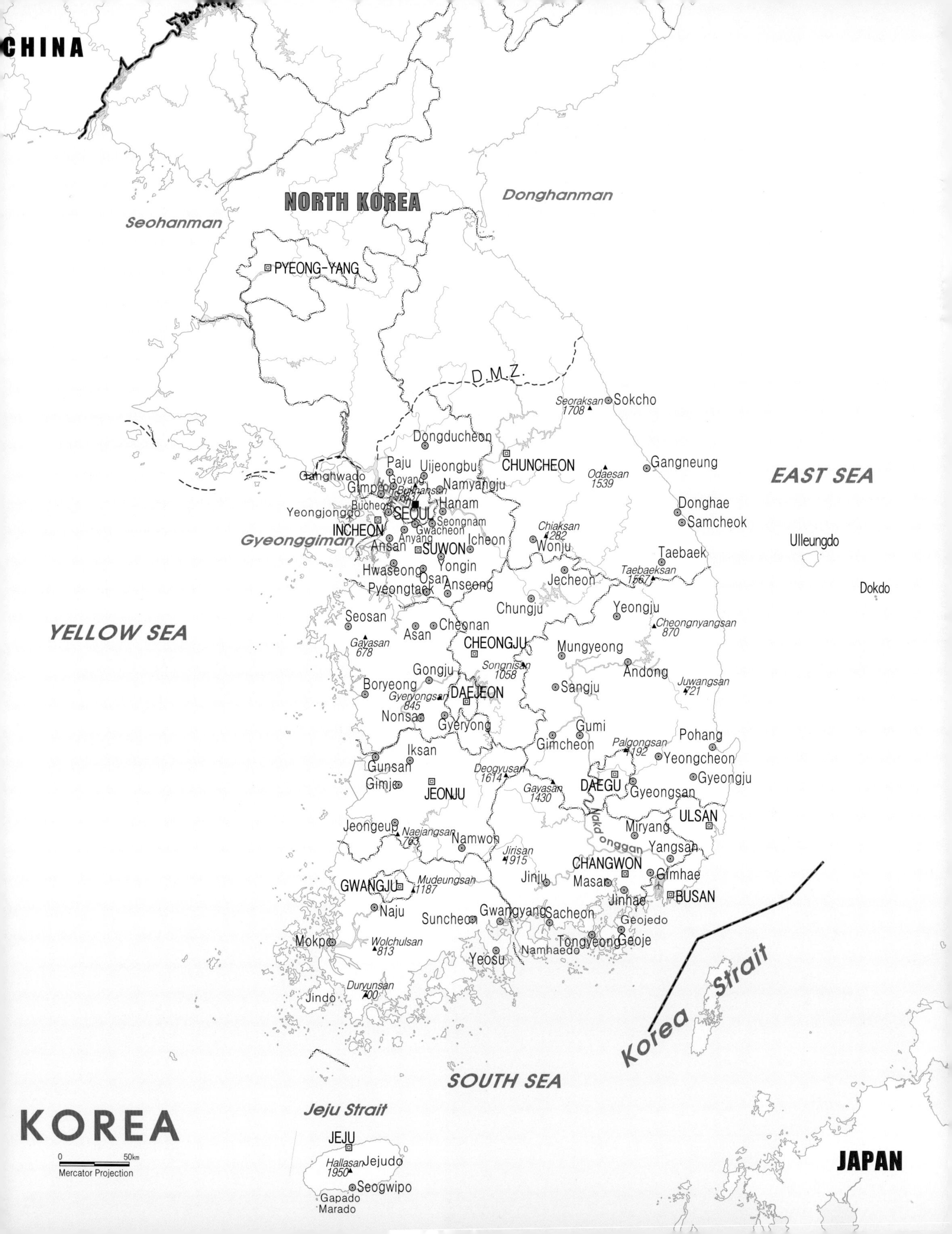
KOREA
CHINA
NORTH KOREA
Seohanman
Donghanman
PYEONG-YANG
D.M.Z.
Seoraksan 1708
Sokcho
Dongducheon
CHUNCHEON
Gangneung
Odaesan 1539
EAST SEA
Paju
Uijeongbu
Ganghwado
Goyang
Gimpo
Bukhansan
Namyangju
Hanam
Bucheon
Yeongjongdo
SEOUL
Seongnam
INCHEON
Gwacheon
Anyang
Gyeonggiman
Ansan
SUWON
Icheon
Chiaksan 1282
Wonju
Donghae
Samcheok
Ulleungdo
Taebaek
Hwaseong
Yongin
Osan
Anseong
Pyeongtaek
Jecheon
Taebaeksan 1567
Dokdo
Chungju
Yeongju
Seosan
YELLOW SEA
Asan
Cheonan
Cheongnyangsan 870
Gayasan 678
CHEONGJU
Mungyeong
Gongju
Songnisan 1058
Andong
Boryeong
Gyeryongsan 845
DAEJEON
Sangju
Juwangsan 721
Nonsan
Gyeryong
Gumi
Gimcheon
Palgongsan 1192
Pohang
Iksan
Yeongcheon
Gunsan
Gimje
JEONJU
Deogyusan 1614
Gayasan 1430
DAEGU
Gyeongsan
Gyeongju
ULSAN
Jeongeup
Naejangsan 763
Namwon
Nakdonggang
Miryang
Yangsan
Jirisan 1915
CHANGWON
Gimhae
GWANGJU
Mudeungsan 1187
Jinju
Masan
Jinhae
BUSAN
Naju
Suncheon
Gwangyang
Sacheon
Geojedo
Mokpo
Wolchulsan 813
Tongyeong
Geoje
Yeosu
Namhaedo
Duryunsan 700
Jindo
Korea Strait
SOUTH SEA
Jeju Strait
JEJU
Hallasan 1950
Jejudo
Seogwipo
Gapado
Marado
0
50km
Mercator Projection
JAPAN

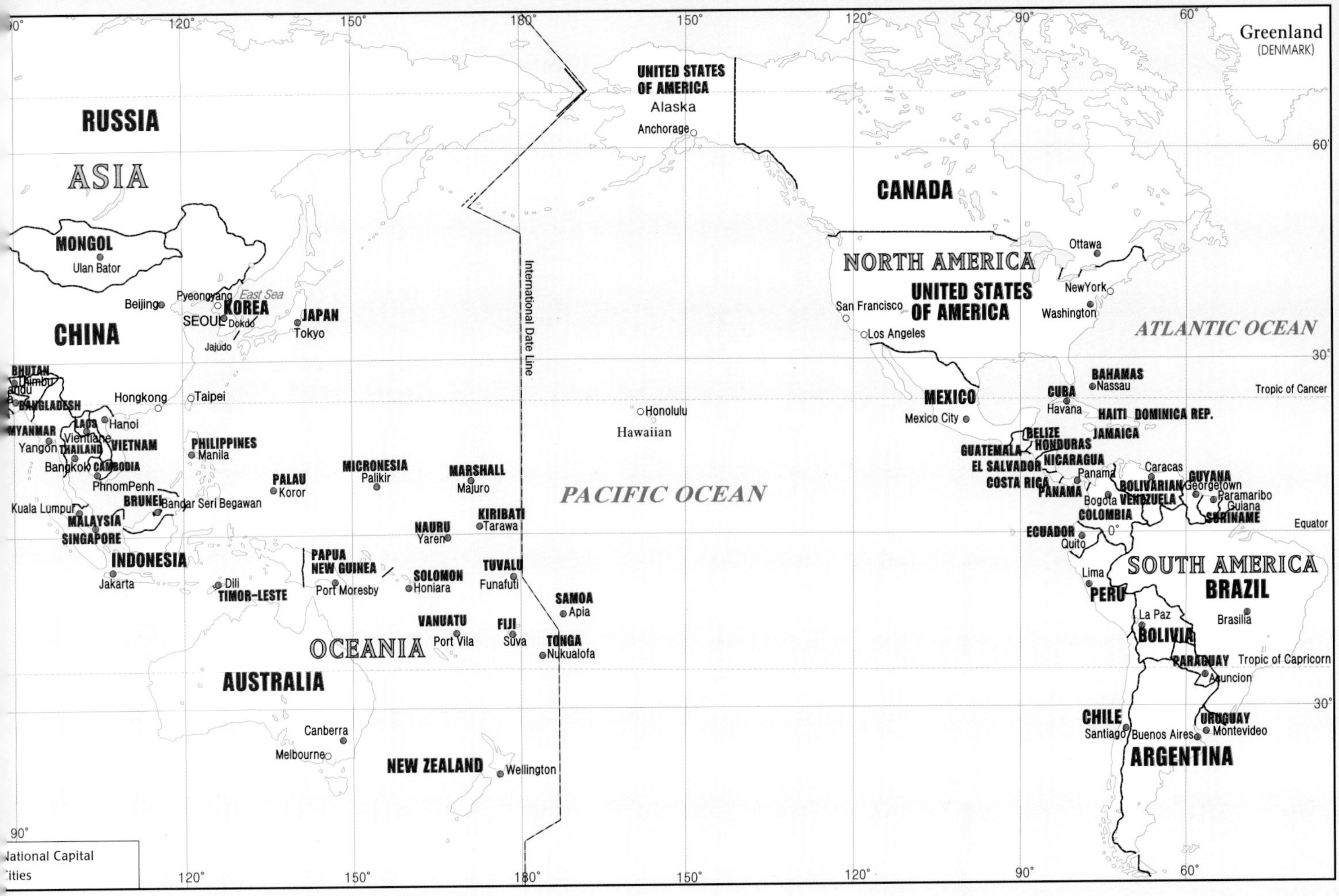

Protruding southeastward from the northeastern corner of the Asian continent, the Republic of Korea has approximately 3,200 islands in its territory. Situated between 33 ° and 43 ° North Latitude and 124 ° and 132 ° East Longitude, Korea is a cold-temperate climate with a standard meridian of 135, nine hours ahead of GMT. The Yalu River and Tumen River border both China and Russia to the north, while Japan is just across the East Sea to the south. Since the 1953 Armistice Agreement following the Korean War, the peninsula has been divided into the Republic of Korea, or South Korea, and the Democratic People's Republic of Korea, or North Korea.

ABOUT THE AUTHOR

A documentary photographer dedicated to capturing with his camera the beauty of Korea, Suh Jae-sik has won over 50 prestigious awards at home and abroad. For his outstanding photography, he received the "Ministry of Culture and Tourism Prize" at the competition under the auspices of the Korea National Tourism Organization. Once worked as a photographer at Hanguk Hwabo and the magazine Seoul, he is a member of the Korea Photographers' Association.

He has been active in publishing picture books. In 1998, he released "The Beauty of Korea" designed to make the nation's unique beauty known worldwide. In 1999, he was responsible for photographs of "Hanoak," a book which exhibited traditional housing culture of Korea, and for this remarkable work he won the "Hankuk Baeksang Publishing Culture Grand Prix" that was granted by the Hankuk Ilbo Daily Newspaper. Also, he was the photographer of "Sweet Place for Living," a magazine released by Goyang City, and "Taekwondo," a book on the nation's martial art which has increasingly become popular around the world. His photographs are also found in "The Thirty-Year History of POSCO," and many corporate brochures of Hanwha Chemical Corp. In his photography book "The Beauty of Seoul," Mr. Suh provides typical images of the capital city, and in "World Heritage in Korea," he displays the fascinating uniqueness of the country's cultural properties which are drawing a keener attention internationally. Also, he released the book "Pillowcases" by collecting his photographs of pillowcases with folk embroidery on them.

More recently, he published books that offered glimpses of the nation's past and future. Among them are "Korean Living Culture" that depicts the country's traditional customs, food and clothing, and "Space Culture in Traditional Korean Homes" which shows esthetics and philosophy in the country's housing culture. Also, he is the photographer of the books "Beautiful Korean Food" and "The Patterns in Korea."

He will remain committed to publicizing Korea overseas by capturing the nation's fascinating beauty and locating its vanishing cultural heritage.

Cellular Phone: 011-891-8088
E-mail: sjaesik@hanmail.net